in larger freedom

TOWARDS DEVELOPMENT, SECURITY AND HUMAN RIGHTS FOR ALL

Report of the Secretary-General

To Mr & Mrs Ewong & Nelly Inglis.

from Lucksheen.

Many thanks for agreeing to be our Chair!

22/5/05

United Nations
New York, 2005

Contents

I. Introduction:
a historic opportunity in 2005

I. Introduction: a historic opportunity in 2005

1. Five years into the new millennium, we have it in our power to pass on to our children a brighter inheritance than that bequeathed to any previous generation. We can halve global poverty and halt the spread of major known diseases in the next 10 years. We can reduce the prevalence of violent conflict and terrorism. We can increase respect for human dignity in every land. And we can forge a set of updated international institutions to help humanity achieve these noble goals. If we act boldly — and if we act together — we can make people everywhere more secure, more prosperous and better able to enjoy their fundamental human rights.

2. All the conditions are in place for us to do so. In an era of global interdependence, the glue of common interest, if properly perceived, should bind all States together in this cause, as should the impulses of our common humanity. In an era of global abundance, our world has the resources to reduce dramatically the massive divides that persist between rich and poor, if only those resources can be unleashed in the service of all peoples. After a period of difficulty in international affairs, in the face of both new threats and old ones in new guises, there is a yearning in many quarters for a new consensus on which to base collective action. And a desire exists to make the most far-reaching reforms in the history of the United Nations so as to equip and resource it to help advance this twenty-first-century agenda.

3. The year 2005 presents an opportunity to move decisively in this direction. In September, world leaders will come together in New York to review progress made since the United Nations Millennium Declaration,[1] adopted by all Member States in 2000. In preparation for that summit, Member States have asked me to report comprehensively on the implementation of the Millennium Declaration. I respectfully submit that report today. I annex to it a proposed agenda to be taken up, and acted upon, at the summit.

4. In preparing the present report, I have drawn on my eight years' experience as Secretary-General, on my own conscience and convictions, and on my understanding of the Charter of the United Nations whose principles and purposes it is my duty to promote. I have also drawn inspiration from two wide-ranging reviews of our global challenges — one from the 16-member High-level Panel on Threats, Challenges and Change, whom I asked to make proposals to strengthen our collective security system (see A/59/565); the other from the 250 experts who undertook the Millennium Project, which required them to produce a plan of action to achieve the Millennium Development Goals by 2015.

5. In the present report, I have resisted the temptation to include all areas in which progress is important or desirable. I have limited myself to items on which I believe action is both vital and achievable in the coming months. These are reforms that are within reach — reforms that are actionable if we can garner the necessary polit-

ical will. With very few exceptions, this is an agenda of highest priorities for September. Many other issues will need to be advanced in other forums and on other occasions. And, of course, none of the proposals advanced here obviate the need for urgent action this year to make progress in resolving protracted conflicts that threaten regional and global stability.

A. THE CHALLENGES OF A CHANGING WORLD

6. In the Millennium Declaration, world leaders were confident that humanity could, in the years ahead, make measurable progress towards peace, security, disarmament, human rights, democracy and good governance. They called for a global partnership for development to achieve agreed goals by 2015. They vowed to protect the vulnerable and meet the special needs of Africa. And they agreed that the United Nations needed to become more, not less, actively engaged in shaping our common future.

7. Five years later, a point-by-point report on the implementation of the Millennium Declaration would, I feel, miss the larger point, namely, that new circumstances demand that we revitalize consensus on key challenges and priorities and convert that consensus into collective action.

8. Much has happened since the adoption of the Millennium Declaration to compel such an approach. Small networks of non-State actors — terrorists — have, since the horrendous attacks of 11 September 2001, made even the most powerful States feel vulnerable. At the same time, many States have begun to feel that the sheer imbalance of power in the world is a source of instability. Divisions between major powers on key issues have revealed a lack of consensus about goals and methods. Meanwhile, over 40 countries have been scarred by violent conflict. Today, the number of internally displaced people stands at roughly 25 million, nearly one third of whom are beyond the reach of United Nations assistance, in addition to the global refugee population of 11-12 million, and some of them have been the victims of war crimes and crimes against humanity.

9. Many countries have been torn apart and hollowed out by violence of a different sort. HIV/AIDS, the plague of the modern world, has killed over 20 million men, women and children and the number of people infected has surged to over 40 million. The promise of the Millennium Development Goals still remains distant for many. More than one billion people still live below the extreme poverty line of one dollar per day, and 20,000 die from poverty each day. Overall global wealth has grown but is less and less evenly distributed within countries, within regions and in the world as a whole. While there has been real progress towards some of the Goals in some countries, too few Governments — from both the developed and the developing world — have taken sufficient action to reach the targets by 2015. And while important work has been done on issues as diverse as migration and climate change,

the scale of such long-term challenges is far greater than our collective action to date to meet them.

10. Events in recent years have also led to declining public confidence in the United Nations itself, even if for opposite reasons. For instance, both sides of the debate on the Iraq war feel let down by the Organization — for failing, as one side saw it, to enforce its own resolutions, or, as the other side saw it, for not being able to prevent a premature or unnecessary war. Yet most people who criticize the United Nations do so precisely because they think the Organization is vitally important to our world. Declining confidence in the institution is matched by a growing belief in the importance of effective multilateralism.

11. I do not suggest that there has been no good news in the last five years. On the contrary, there is plenty we can point to which demonstrates that collective action can produce real results, from the impressive unity of the world after 11 September 2001 to the resolution of a number of civil conflicts, and from the appreciable increase of resources for development to the steady progress achieved in building peace and democracy in some war-torn lands. We should never despair. Our problems are not beyond our power to meet them. But we cannot be content with incomplete successes and we cannot make do with incremental responses to the shortcomings that have been revealed. Instead, we must come together to bring about far-reaching change.

B. LARGER FREEDOM: DEVELOPMENT, SECURITY AND HUMAN RIGHTS

12. Our guiding light must be the needs and hopes of peoples everywhere. In my Millennium Report, "We the peoples" (A/54/2000), I drew on the opening words of the Charter of the United Nations to point out that the United Nations, while it is an organization of sovereign States, exists for and must ultimately serve those needs. To do so, we must aim, as I said when first elected eight years ago, "to perfect the triangle of development, freedom and peace".

13. The framers of the Charter saw this very clearly. In setting out to save succeeding generations from the scourge of war, they understood that this enterprise could not succeed if it was narrowly based. They therefore decided to create an organization to ensure respect for fundamental human rights, establish conditions under which justice and the rule of law could be maintained, and "promote social progress and better standards of life in larger freedom".

14. I have named the present report "In larger freedom" to stress the enduring relevance of the Charter of the United Nations and to emphasize that its purposes must be advanced in the lives of individual men and women. The notion of larger freedom also encapsulates the idea that development, security and human rights go hand in hand.

15.   Even if he can vote to choose his rulers, a young man with AIDS who cannot read or write and lives on the brink of starvation is not truly free. Equally, even if she earns enough to live, a woman who lives in the shadow of daily violence and has no say in how her country is run is not truly free. Larger freedom implies that men and women everywhere have the right to be governed by their own consent, under law, in a society where all individuals can, without discrimination or retribution, speak, worship and associate freely. They must also be free from want — so that the death sentences of extreme poverty and infectious disease are lifted from their lives — and free from fear — so that their lives and livelihoods are not ripped apart by violence and war. Indeed, all people have the right to security and to development.

16.   Not only are development, security and human rights all imperative; they also reinforce each other. This relationship has only been strengthened in our era of rapid technological advances, increasing economic interdependence, globalization and dramatic geopolitical change. While poverty and denial of human rights may not be said to "cause" civil war, terrorism or organized crime, they all greatly increase the risk of instability and violence. Similarly, war and atrocities are far from the only reasons that countries are trapped in poverty, but they undoubtedly set back development. Again, catastrophic terrorism on one side of the globe, for example an attack against a major financial centre in a rich country, could affect the development prospects of millions on the other by causing a major economic downturn and plunging millions into poverty. And countries which are well governed and respect the human rights of their citizens are better placed to avoid the horrors of conflict and to overcome obstacles to development.

17.   Accordingly, we will not enjoy development without security, we will not enjoy security without development, and we will not enjoy either without respect for human rights. Unless all these causes are advanced, none will succeed. In this new millennium, the work of the United Nations must move our world closer to the day when all people have the freedom to choose the kind of lives they would like to live, the access to the resources that would make those choices meaningful and the security to ensure that they can be enjoyed in peace.

C. THE IMPERATIVE OF COLLECTIVE ACTION

18.   In a world of interconnected threats and challenges, it is in each country's self-interest that all of them are addressed effectively. Hence, the cause of larger freedom can only be advanced by broad, deep and sustained global cooperation among States. Such cooperation is possible if every country's policies take into account not only the needs of its own citizens but also the needs of others. This kind of cooperation not only advances everyone's interests but also recognizes our common humanity.

19.   The proposals contained in the present report are designed to strengthen States and enable them to serve their peoples better by working together on the basis of shared

principles and priorities — which is, after all, the very reason the United Nations exists. Sovereign States are the basic and indispensable building blocks of the international system. It is their job to guarantee the rights of their citizens, to protect them from crime, violence and aggression, and to provide the framework of freedom under law in which individuals can prosper and society develop. If States are fragile, the peoples of the world will not enjoy the security, development and justice that are their right. Therefore, one of the great challenges of the new millennium is to ensure that all States are strong enough to meet the many challenges they face.

20. States, however, cannot do the job alone. We need an active civil society and a dynamic private sector. Both occupy an increasingly large and important share of the space formerly reserved for States alone, and it is plain that the goals outlined here will not be achieved without their full engagement.

21. We also need agile and effective regional and global intergovernmental institutions to mobilize and coordinate collective action. As the world's only universal body with a mandate to address security, development and human rights issues, the United Nations bears a special burden. As globalization shrinks distances around the globe and these issues become increasingly interconnected, the comparative advantages of the United Nations become ever more evident. So too, however, do some of its real weaknesses. From overhauling basic management practices and building a more transparent, efficient and effective United Nations system to revamping our major intergovernmental institutions so that they reflect today's world and advance the priorities set forth in the present report, we must reshape the Organization in ways not previously imagined and with a boldness and speed not previously shown.

22. In our efforts to strengthen the contributions of States, civil society, the private sector and international institutions to advancing a vision of larger freedom, we must ensure that all involved assume their responsibilities to turn good words into good deeds. We therefore need new mechanisms to ensure accountability — the accountability of States to their citizens, of States to each other, of international institutions to their members and of the present generation to future generations. Where there is accountability we will progress; where there is none we will underperform. The business of the summit to be held in September 2005 must be to ensure that, from now on, promises made are promises kept.

D. Time to decide

23. At this defining moment in history, we must be ambitious. Our action must be as urgent as the need, and on the same scale. We must face immediate threats immediately. We must take advantage of an unprecedented consensus on how to promote global economic and social development, and we must forge a new consensus on how to confront new threats. Only by acting decisively now can we both confront

the pressing security challenges and win a decisive victory in the global battle against poverty by 2015.

24.   In today's world, no State, however powerful, can protect itself on its own. Likewise, no country, weak or strong, can realize prosperity in a vacuum. We can and must act together. We owe it to each other to do so, and we owe each other an account of how we do so. If we live up to those mutual commitments, we can make the new millennium worthy of its name.

II. Freedom from want

II. Freedom from want

25. The past 25 years have seen the most dramatic reduction in extreme poverty that the world has ever experienced. Spearheaded by progress in China and India, literally hundreds of millions of men, women and children all over the world have been able to escape the burdens of extreme impoverishment and begin to enjoy improved access to food, health care, education and housing.

26. Yet at the same time, dozens of countries have become poorer, devastating economic crises have thrown millions of families into poverty, and increasing inequality in large parts of the world means that the benefits of economic growth have not been evenly shared. Today, more than a billion people — one in every six human beings — still live on less than a dollar a day, lacking the means to stay alive in the face of chronic hunger, disease and environmental hazards. In other words, this is a poverty that kills. A single bite from a malaria-bearing mosquito is enough to end a child's life for want of a bed net or $1 treatment. A drought or pest that destroys a harvest turns subsistence into starvation. A world in which every year 11 million children die before their fifth birthday and 3 million people die of AIDS is not a world of larger freedom.

27. For centuries, this kind of poverty has been regarded as a sad but inescapable aspect of the human condition. Today, that view is intellectually and morally indefensible. The scale and scope of progress made by countries in every region of the world have shown that, over a very short time, poverty and maternal and infant mortality can be dramatically reduced, while education, gender equality and other aspects of development can be dramatically advanced. The unprecedented combination of resources and technology at our disposal today means that we are truly the first generation with the tools, the knowledge and the resources to meet the commitment, given by all States in the Millennium Declaration, "to making the right to development a reality for everyone and to freeing the entire human race from want".

A. A SHARED VISION OF DEVELOPMENT

28. The multifaceted challenge of development cuts across a vast array of interlinked issues — ranging from gender equality through health and education to the environment. The historic United Nations conferences and summits held in the 1990s helped build a comprehensive normative framework around these linkages for the first time by mapping out a broad vision of shared development priorities. These laid the groundwork for the Millennium Summit to set out a series of time-bound targets across all these areas — ranging from halving extreme poverty to putting all children into primary school, all with a deadline of 2015 — that were later crystallized into the Millennium Development Goals (see box 1).

Box 1

The Millennium Development Goals

Goal 1
ERADICATE EXTREME POVERTY AND HUNGER

Target 1   Halve, between 1990 and 2015, the proportion of people whose income is less than one dollar a day

Target 2   Halve, between 1990 and 2015, the proportion of people who suffer from hunger

Goal 2
ACHIEVE UNIVERSAL PRIMARY EDUCATION

Target 3   Ensure that, by 2015, children everywhere, boys and girls alike, will be able to complete a full course of primary schooling

Goal 3
PROMOTE GENDER EQUALITY AND EMPOWER WOMEN

Target 4   Eliminate gender disparity in primary and secondary education, preferably by 2005, and at all levels of education no later than 2015

Goal 4
REDUCE CHILD MORTALITY

Target 5   Reduce by two thirds, between 1990 and 2015, the under-five mortality rate

Goal 5
IMPROVE MATERNAL HEALTH

Target 6   Reduce by three quarters, between 1990 and 2015, the maternal mortality ratio

Goal 6
COMBAT HIV/AIDS, MALARIA AND OTHER DISEASES

Target 7   Have halted by 2015 and begun to reverse the spread of HIV/AIDS

Target 8   Have halted by 2015 and begun to reverse the incidence of malaria and other major diseases

Goal 7
ENSURE ENVIRONMENTAL SUSTAINABILITY

Target 9   Integrate the principles of sustainable development into country policies and programmes and reverse the loss of environmental resources

Target 10	Halve, by 2015, the proportion of people without sustainable access to safe drinking water and basic sanitation
Target 11	Achieve, by 2020, a significant improvement in the lives of at least 100 million slum-dwellers

Goal 8
DEVELOP A GLOBAL PARTNERSHIP FOR DEVELOPMENT

Target 12	Develop further an open, rule-based, predictable, non-discriminatory trading and financial system (includes a commitment to good governance, development and poverty reduction — both nationally and internationally)
Target 13	Address the special needs of the least developed countries (includes tariff- and quota-free access for least developed countries exports; enhanced programme of debt relief for heavily indebted poor countries and cancellation of official bilateral debt; and more generous ODA for countries committed to poverty reduction)
Target 14	Address the special needs of landlocked countries and small island developing States (through the Programme of Action for the Sustainable Development of Small Island Developing States and the outcome of the twenty-second special session of the General Assembly)
Target 15	Deal comprehensively with the debt problems of developing countries through national and international measures in order to make debt sustainable in the long term
Target 16	In cooperation with developing countries, develop and implement strategies for decent and productive work for youth
Target 17	In cooperation with pharmaceutical companies, provide access to affordable, essential drugs in developing countries
Target 18	In cooperation with the private sector, make available the benefits of new technologies, especially information and communications

29. The Millennium Development Goals have galvanized unprecedented efforts to meet the needs of the world's poorest, becoming globally accepted benchmarks of broader progress embraced by donors, developing countries, civil society and major development institutions alike. As such, they reflect an urgent and globally shared and endorsed set of priorities that we need to address at the September 2005 summit. Thanks to the work done by the Millennium Project, whose report, *Investing in Development: A Practical Plan to Achieve the Millennium Development Goals*,[2] was delivered to me in January 2005, there is now an action plan to achieve them. There are also encouraging signs that the critical ingredient — political will — is emerging. The real test will be whether broad-based actions by developed and developing

countries to address this agenda are supported by more than doubling global development assistance over the next few years, for this is what will be necessary to help achieve the Goals.

30.   At the same time, we need to see the Millennium Development Goals as part of an even larger development agenda. While the Goals have been the subject of an enormous amount of follow-up both inside and outside the United Nations, they clearly do not in themselves represent a complete development agenda. They do not directly encompass some of the broader issues covered by the conferences of the 1990s, nor do they address the particular needs of middle-income developing countries or the questions of growing inequality and the wider dimensions of human development and good governance, which all require the effective implementation of conference outcomes.

31.   Nevertheless, the urgency of achieving the Millennium Development Goals cannot be overstated. Despite progress in many areas, overall the world is falling short of what is needed, especially in the poorest countries (see box 2). As the Millennium Project's report makes clear, our agenda is still achievable globally and in most or even all countries — but only if we break with business as usual and dramatically accelerate and scale up action until 2015, beginning over the next 12 months. Success will require sustained action across the entire decade between now and the deadline. That is because development successes cannot take place overnight and many countries suffer significant capacity constraints. It takes time to train the teachers, nurses and engineers, to build the roads, schools and hospitals, and to grow the small and large businesses able to create the jobs and income needed.

32.   In 2005, the development of a global partnership between rich and poor countries — which is itself the eighth Goal, reaffirmed and elaborated three years ago at the International Conference on Financing for Development, held in Monterrey, Mexico, and the World Summit on Sustainable Development, held in Johannesburg, South Africa — needs to become a reality. It is worth recalling the terms of that historic compact. **Each developing country has primary responsibility for its own development — strengthening governance, combating corruption and putting in place the policies and investments to drive private sector–led growth and maximize the domestic resources available to fund national development strategies. Developed countries, on their side, undertake that developing countries which adopt transparent, credible and properly costed development strategies will receive the full support they need, in the form of increased development assistance, a more development-oriented trade system and wider and deeper debt relief.** All of this has been promised but not delivered. That failure is measured in the rolls of the dead — and on it are written millions of new names each year.

Box 2

Progress on the Millennium Development Goals

Progress in achieving the Millennium Development Goals has been far from uniform across the world. The greatest improvements have been in East Asia and South Asia, where more than 200 million people have been lifted out of poverty since 1990 alone. Nonetheless, nearly 700 million people in Asia still live on less than $1 a day — nearly two thirds of the world's poorest people — while even some of the fastest-growing countries are falling short on non-income Goals, such as protecting the environment and reducing maternal mortality. Sub-Saharan Africa is at the epicentre of the crisis, falling seriously short on most Goals, with continuing food insecurity, disturbingly high child and maternal mortality, growing numbers of people living in slums and an overall rise of extreme poverty despite some important progress in individual countries. Latin America, the transition economies, and the Middle East and North Africa, often hampered by growing inequality, have more mixed records, with significant variations in progress but general trends falling short of what is needed to meet the 2015 deadline.

Progress in the achievement of the different Goals has also varied. Although sub-Saharan Africa and Oceania are lagging in almost all areas, elsewhere major advances are being made in reducing hunger, improving access to drinking water and expanding the number of children in primary school. Child mortality rates have also generally declined, but progress has slowed in many regions and has even been reversed in parts of Central Asia. Meanwhile, despite dramatic progress in some countries overall access to sanitation is off track, particularly in Africa and Asia, where the number of slum-dwellers is also increasing rapidly. Maternal mortality remains unacceptably high throughout the developing world, as do the incidence and prevalence of HIV/AIDS, tuberculosis and malaria. Gender equality remains unfulfilled; the 2005 education parity target was missed in many countries. Environmental degradation is an extreme concern in all developing regions.

B. National strategies

33.   Extreme poverty has many causes, ranging from adverse geography through poor or corrupt governance (including neglect of marginalized communities) to the ravages of conflict and its aftermath. Most pernicious are poverty traps that leave many of the poorest countries languishing in a vicious circle of destitution even when they have the benefit of honest, committed Governments. Lacking basic infrastructure, human capital and public administration, and burdened by disease, environmental degradation and limited natural resources, these countries cannot afford the basic investments needed to move onto a new path of prosperity unless they receive sustained, targeted external support.

34. As a first step towards addressing these problems, countries need to adopt bold, goal-oriented policy frameworks for the next 10 years, aimed at scaling up investments to achieve at least the quantitative Millennium Development Goals targets. **To that end, each developing country with extreme poverty should by 2006 adopt and begin to implement a national development strategy bold enough to meet the Millennium Development Goals targets for 2015.** This strategy should be anchored in the practical scaling up of public investments, capacity-building, domestic resource mobilization and, where needed, official development assistance. This recommendation may not sound revolutionary, but by linking actions directly to the needs derived from ambitious and monitorable targets, its implementation would mark a fundamental breakthrough towards greater boldness and accountability in the fight against poverty.

35. It is important to stress that this does not require the creation of any new instruments. All that is required is a different approach to their design and implementation. Countries that already have poverty reduction strategy papers — nationally owned and developed three-year spending frameworks agreed with the World Bank and other international development partners — should align them with a 10-year framework of policies and investments consistent with achievement of the Millennium Development Goals. In middle-income countries and others where the Goals are already within reach, Governments should adopt a "Millennium Development Goals–plus" strategy, with more ambitious targets.

A framework for action

36. However well crafted on paper, investment strategies to achieve the Millennium Development Goals will not work in practice unless supported by States with transparent, accountable systems of governance, grounded in the rule of law, encompassing civil and political as well as economic and social rights, and underpinned by accountable and efficient public administration. Many of the poorest countries will need major capacity-building investments to put in place and maintain the necessary infrastructure and to train and employ qualified personnel. But without good governance, strong institutions and a clear commitment to rooting out corruption and mismanagement wherever it is found, broader progress will prove elusive.

37. Similarly, without dynamic, growth-oriented economic policies supporting a healthy private sector capable of generating jobs, income and tax revenues over time, sustainable economic growth will not be achieved. This requires significantly increased investments in human capital and development-oriented infrastructure, such as energy, transport and communications. In addition, small and medium-sized firms require a favourable legal and regulatory environment, including effective commercial laws that define and protect contracts and property rights, a rational public administration that limits and combats corruption, and expanded

access to financial capital, including microfinance. As two important commissions — the World Commission on the Social Dimension of Globalization[3] and the Commission on the Private Sector and Development[4] — reported to me last year, this is crucial for providing decent jobs that both provide income and empower the poor, especially women and younger people.

38. Civil society organizations have a critical role to play in driving this implementation process forward to "make poverty history". Not only is civil society an indispensable partner in delivering services to the poor at the scope required by the Millennium Development Goals but it can also catalyse action within countries on pressing development concerns, mobilizing broad-based movements and creating grass-roots pressure to hold leaders accountable for their commitments. Internationally, some civil society organizations can help create or galvanize global partnerships on specific issues or draw attention to the plight of indigenous peoples and other marginalized groups, while others can work to share best practices across countries through community exchanges and providing technical support and advice to Governments.

National investment and policy priorities

39. Each national strategy needs to take into account seven broad "clusters" of public investments and policies which directly address the Millennium Development Goals and set the foundation for private sector–led growth. As elaborated in the Millennium Project, all are essential for meeting the Goals, as well as wider development needs.

Gender equality: overcoming pervasive gender bias

40. Empowered women can be some of the most effective drivers of development. Direct interventions to advance gender equality include increasing primary school completion and secondary school access for girls, ensuring secure tenure of property to women, ensuring access to sexual and reproductive health services, promoting equal access to labour markets, providing the opportunity for greater representation in government decision-making bodies and protecting women from violence.

The environment: investing in better resource management

41. Countries should adopt time-bound environmental targets, particularly for such priorities as forest replanting, integrated water resources management, ecosystem preservation and curbing pollution. To achieve targets, increased investments in environmental management need to be accompanied by broad policy reforms. Progress also depends on sector strategies, including strategies for agriculture, infrastructure, forestry, fisheries, energy and transport, which all require environmental safeguards. Further, improving access to modern energy services is critical for both reducing poverty and protecting the environment. There is also a need to ensure

that enhancing access to safe drinking water and sanitation forms a part of development strategies.

Rural development: increasing food output and incomes

42. Smallholder farmers and others living in impoverished rural areas require soil nutrients, better plant varieties, improved water management and training in modern and environmentally sustainable farming practices, along with access to transport, water, sanitation and modern energy services. **In sub-Saharan Africa, these elements must be brought together to launch a twenty-first-century African green revolution commencing in 2005.**

Urban development: promoting jobs, upgrading slums and developing alternatives to new slum formation

43. For the large and growing number of urban poor, core infrastructure services, such as energy, transport, pollution control and waste disposal, are needed alongside improved security of tenure and community-led efforts to build decent housing and support urban planning. To this end, local authorities need to be strengthened and work closely with organizations of the urban poor.

Health systems: ensuring universal access to essential services

44. Strong health systems are required to ensure universal access to basic health services, including services to promote child and maternal health, to support reproductive health and to control killer diseases, such as AIDS, tuberculosis and malaria (see box 3). This requires sufficient investments, large numbers of motivated and adequately paid health workers, scaled-up infrastructure and supplies, strong management systems and the elimination of user fees.

Education: ensuring universal primary, expanded secondary and higher education

45. To advance education at all levels, parents and communities should be able to hold their schools accountable while Governments improve curricula, educational quality and mode of delivery; build human resource and infrastructure capacity, where needed; and institute incentives for bringing vulnerable children to school, including the elimination of user fees.

Science, technology and innovation: building national capacities

46. To increase countries' indigenous capacity for science and technology, including information and communications technology, Governments should establish scientific advisory bodies, promote infrastructure as an opportunity for technological learning, expand science and engineering faculties, and stress development and business applications in science and technology curricula.

Box 3

The tragedy of HIV/AIDS

The HIV/AIDS pandemic now kills more than 3 million people each year and poses an unprecedented threat to human development and security. The disease is wrecking millions of families and leaving tens of millions of orphans. More than just a public health crisis, AIDS undermines economic and social stability, ravaging health, education, agriculture and social welfare systems. While placing an enormous drag on economic growth, it also weakens governance and security structures, posing a further threat.

The epidemic demands an exceptional response. In the absence of a cure, only the mass mobilization of every section of society — unheard of to date in the history of public health — can begin to reverse AIDS. This requires comprehensive prevention, education, treatment and impact mitigation programmes, which in turn will not succeed without the personal commitment of Heads of State and Government to support and lead genuinely multisectoral AIDS responses.

Since 2000, the world has begun to achieve some successes in the fight against AIDS. More Governments have made it a strategic priority and set up integrated administrative structures to lead and coordinate the struggle. The Global Fund to Fight AIDS, Tuberculosis and Malaria, which I called for in 2001, now plays a leading role in the global effort, while also focusing attention on and fighting other killer pandemics. Altogether, as of December 2004, 700,000 people in the developing world were receiving antiretroviral treatment — a nearly 60 per cent increase in just five months. This reflects the priority that the international community has now placed on rapidly expanding treatment, and shows that a real difference can be made in a very short time.

However, much remains to be done if we are to have any realistic hope of reducing the incidence of HIV and providing proper antiretroviral treatment to all who need it within the coming decade. Many Governments have yet to tackle the disease and its stigma publicly, or are not sufficiently committed to the kind of frank discussion and action on gender equality that is needed. In particular, resources for AIDS remain far short of what is needed to mount a full inclusive response. National Governments, as well as multilateral and bilateral donors, must now take steps to meet these costs.

Four years ago, I called on the international community to provide $7 billion to $10 billion annually to address the projected needs to fight HIV/AIDS in the developing world. This amount has not been fully funded. In the meantime, the disease has spread. As a result, we have an ever-increasing gap between what is needed and what is provided. This cannot continue. We need a more ambitious and balanced strategy of both prevention and treatment. **Therefore, I call on the international community to provide urgently the resources needed for an expanded and comprehensive response to HIV/AIDS, as identified by the Joint United Nations Programme on HIV/AIDS (UNAIDS) and its partners, and to provide full funding for the Global Fund to Fight AIDS, Tuberculosis and Malaria.**

C. MAKING GOAL 8 WORK: TRADE AND FINANCING FOR DEVELOPMENT

47. For many middle-income countries and some poorer ones, most of the resources needed to fund these strategies can and should be mobilized domestically from re-allocated government revenues, household contributions and private sector investment, supplemented by borrowing. But in most low-income countries and in nearly all the least developed countries, the maximum that can be raised by such efforts will fall far short of what is needed to reach the Millennium Development Goals. According to the Millennium Project, the investment costs for the Goals alone in a typical low-income country will be roughly $75 per capita in 2006, rising to approximately $140 in 2015 (in constant dollar terms). These small sums, equivalent to one third to one half of their annual per capita incomes, are far beyond the resources of most low-income countries. To create the conditions for greater private investment and an "exit strategy" from aid in the longer term for these countries, a big push in development assistance is needed.

Aid

48. One of the most encouraging shifts in recent years has been the increase in official development assistance (ODA), after a decade of steady decline in the 1990s. Expressed as a percentage of developed countries' gross national income, global ODA currently stands at 0.25 per cent — still well short of the 0.33 per cent reached in the late 1980s, let alone the long-standing target of 0.7 per cent that was reaffirmed in the Monterrey Consensus in 2002.[5] On the basis of recent commitments to future increases by several donors, annual ODA flows should increase to about $100 billion by 2010 — nearly double their levels at the time of the Monterrey Conference. But a significant portion of this amount reflects debt write-offs and dollar depreciation rather than net long-term finance, and in any case the total would still be about $50 billion short of the ODA levels that the Millennium Project calculates will be needed just to meet the Millennium Development Goals, let alone broader development priorities.

49. Happily, there are signs of further progress. A new group of donors has emerged, including new members of the European Union (EU) and some of the wealthier developing countries, such as Brazil, China and India, all of which are increasingly offering their expertise to other developing countries through technical cooperation. Five donor countries have already reached the 0.7 per cent target and six more have recently set timetables to achieve it. **Developed countries that have not already done so should establish timetables to achieve the 0.7 per cent target of gross national income for official development assistance by no later than 2015, starting with significant increases no later than 2006 and reaching 0.5 per cent by 2009.**

50. While there are clearly capacity constraints in many developing countries, we must ensure that those countries that are ready receive an immediate scale-up in as-

sistance. **Starting in 2005, developing countries that put forward sound, transparent and accountable national strategies and require increased development assistance should receive a sufficient increase in aid, of sufficient quality and arriving with sufficient speed to enable them to achieve the Millennium Development Goals.**

51.   The most direct way to increase ODA volumes is to allocate increasing shares of donor countries' national budgets to aid. However, because the achievement of the Millennium Development Goals requires a sharp upward turn in overall ODA spending over the next few years, new ways to finance a steep increase in the short and medium terms are well worth exploring. Several longer-term ideas for innovative sources of finance to complement ODA have been proposed, and an important initiative led by Brazil, Chile, France, Germany and Spain is currently exploring some of them. But what is needed now is a mechanism to ensure the immediate scale-up of financing. The proposed International Finance Facility has the potential to do this by "front-loading" future flows of ODA while still using existing disbursement channels. **The international community should in 2005 launch an International Finance Facility to support an immediate front-loading of ODA, underpinned by scaled-up commitments to achieving the 0.7 per cent ODA target no later than 2015. In the longer term, other innovative sources of finance for development should also be considered to supplement the Facility.**

52.   **These steps can and should be supplemented by immediate action to support a series of "quick wins" — relatively inexpensive, high-impact initiatives with the potential to generate major short-term gains and save millions of lives.** These range from the free mass distribution of malaria bed nets and effective antimalaria medicines to the expansion of home-grown school meal programmes using locally produced food and the elimination of user fees for primary education and health services. Such rapid steps would provide a critical support for national Millennium Development Goals strategies. They would generate rapid momentum and early success stories that would broaden commitment to the Millennium Development Goals, although they would not be a substitute for longer-term, sustained investments.

53.   At the same time, urgent steps are needed to increase the quality, transparency and accountability of ODA. Aid should be linked to the local needs identified in countries' national strategies and to the achievement of the Millennium Development Goals, not to the interests of suppliers in donor countries. This is obviously for the benefit of developing countries, but developed countries themselves also have an interest in being able to show their taxpayers that aid is effective. **In follow-up to the March 2005 Paris High-level Forum on Aid Effectiveness, donor countries should set, by September 2005, timetables and monitorable targets for aligning their aid delivery mechanisms with partner countries' Millennium Development Goals–based national strategies.** This includes commitments to Millennium Development Goals–based investment plans, a 2015 time-horizon, predictable multi-year funding,

dramatically simplified procedures and direct budget support for countries with appropriate mechanisms in place.

Debt

54. Closely related to ODA is the issue of external debt. Under the Heavily Indebted Poor Countries (HIPC) Initiative, $54 billion has so far been committed for debt relief to 27 countries that have reached decision or completion points. But even though the evidence is persuasive that this unlocks resources which are critical for the Millennium Development Goals, it still falls far short of what is needed. **To move forward, we should redefine debt sustainability as the level of debt that allows a country to achieve the Millennium Development Goals and reach 2015 without an increase in debt ratios.** For most HIPC countries, this will require exclusively grant-based finance and 100 per cent debt cancellation, while for many heavily indebted non-HIPC and middle-income countries it will require significantly more debt reduction than has yet been on offer. Additional debt cancellation should be achieved without reducing the resources available to other developing countries, and without jeopardizing the long-term financial viability of international financial institutions.

Trade

55. While trade does not obviate the need for large scale ODA-supported development investments, an open and equitable trading system can be a powerful driver of economic growth and poverty reduction, especially when combined with adequate aid. Development therefore rightly lies at the heart of the World Trade Organization (WTO) Doha round of multilateral trade negotiations. At present, developing countries are often denied a level playing field to compete in global trade because rich countries use a variety of tariffs, quotas and subsidies to restrict access to their own markets and shelter their own producers. The December 2005 WTO ministerial meeting offers a chance, which must not be missed, to map out agreement on how to correct these anomalies. An urgent priority is to establish a timetable for developed countries to dismantle market access barriers and begin phasing out trade-distorting domestic subsidies, especially in agriculture. **To address this priority, the Doha round of multilateral trade negotiations should fulfil its development promise and be completed no later than 2006. As a first step, Member States should provide duty-free and quota-free market access for all exports from the least developed countries.**

56. The Monterrey Consensus stressed that for many developing countries, particularly the poorest, which rely on a few commodity products, there is also a supply-side problem which manifests itself in a lack of capacity to diversify exports, a vulnerability to price fluctuations and a steady decline in terms of trade. To build trade competitiveness, national Millennium Development Goals strategies need to

emphasize investments in agricultural productivity, trade-related infrastructure and competitive export industries, particularly for the least developed countries, land-locked developing countries and small island developing States. While a number of initiatives exist to address these problems, encourage diversification and reduce vulnerability to commodity price fluctuations, support for them has fallen far short of what is necessary.

D. Ensuring environmental sustainability

57. We fundamentally depend on natural systems and resources for our existence and development. Our efforts to defeat poverty and pursue sustainable development will be in vain if environmental degradation and natural resource depletion continue unabated. At the country level, national strategies must include investments in improved environmental management and make the structural changes required for environmental sustainability. For many environmental priorities, such as shared waterways, forests, marine fisheries and biodiversity, regional and global efforts must be strengthened. We already have one encouraging example showing how global solutions can be found. Thanks to the Montreal Protocol on Substances that Deplete the Ozone Layer,[6] the risk of harmful radiation appears to be receding — a clear demonstration of how global environmental problems can be managed when all countries make determined efforts to implement internationally agreed frameworks. Today, three major challenges for the international community require particularly urgent action, as described below.

Desertification

58. The degradation of more than a billion hectares of land has had a devastating impact on development in many parts of the world. Millions of people have been forced to abandon their lands as farming and nomadic lifestyles have become un-sustainable. Hundreds of millions more are at risk of becoming environmental refugees. To combat desertification, the international community must support and implement the United Nations Convention to Combat Desertification in Those Countries Experiencing Serious Drought and/or Desertification, Particularly in Africa.[7]

Biodiversity

59. Another serious concern is loss of biodiversity, which is occurring at an unprecedented rate within and across countries. Worrying in its own right, this trend also severely undermines health, livelihoods, food production and clean water, and increases the vulnerability of populations to natural disasters and climate change. To reverse these trends, all Governments should take steps, individually and collectively, to implement the Convention on Biological Diversity[8] and the Johannesburg

commitment to achieve a significant reduction in the rate of loss of biodiversity by 2010.[9]

Climate change

60.   One of the greatest environmental and development challenges in the twenty-first century will be that of controlling and coping with climate change. The overwhelming majority of scientists now agree that human activity is having a significant impact on the climate. Since the advent of the industrial era in the mid-eighteenth century, atmospheric concentrations of greenhouse gases have increased significantly, the earth has warmed considerably and sea levels have risen measurably. The 1990s were the warmest decade on record, forcing glaciers and Arctic ice to retreat. With the concentration of greenhouse gases projected to rise still further over the next century, a corresponding increase in the global mean surface temperature is likely to trigger increased climate variability and greater incidence and intensity of extreme weather events, such as hurricanes and droughts. The countries most vulnerable to such changes — small island developing States, coastal nations with large numbers of people living in low-lying areas, and countries in the arid and semi-arid tropics and subtropics — are least able to protect themselves. They also contribute least to the global emissions of greenhouse gases. Without action, they will pay a bitter price for the actions of others.

61.   The entry into force in February 2005 of the 1997 Kyoto Protocol[10] to the United Nations Framework Convention on Climate Change[11] is an important step towards dealing with global warming, but it only extends until 2012. The international community must agree on stabilization targets for greenhouse gas concentrations beyond that date. Scientific advances and technological innovation have an important role to play in mitigating climate change and in facilitating adaptation to the new conditions. They must be mobilized now if we are to develop the tools needed in time. In particular, research and development funding for renewable energy sources, carbon management and energy efficiency needs to increase substantially. Policy mechanisms, such as carbon trading markets, should also be expanded. As agreed at Johannesburg, the primary responsibility for mitigating climate change and other unsustainable patterns of production and consumption must lie with the countries that contribute most to the problems. **We must develop a more inclusive international framework beyond 2012, with broader participation by all major emitters and both developed and developing countries, to ensure a concerted globally defined action, including through technological innovation, to mitigate climate change, taking into account the principle of common but differentiated responsibilities.**

E. Other priorities for global action

62.   To address broader development needs, action is also needed in a number of other areas, as set out below.

Infectious disease surveillance and monitoring

63. The overall international response to evolving pandemics has been shockingly slow and remains shamefully under-resourced. Malaria continues to rage throughout the tropical world, despite the availability of highly effective measures for prevention and treatment. Many infectious diseases that ravage developing countries today, notably HIV/AIDS and tuberculosis, pose severe risks for the entire world, particularly in the light of emerging drug resistance. Both familiar and new infectious diseases require a concerted international response. The severe acute respiratory syndrome (SARS) outbreak of 2003 drew attention to the fact that even long-distance flight times are shorter than the incubation periods for many infectious diseases, so that any one of the 700 million passengers who take international flights each year can be an unwitting disease carrier.

64. The rapid response to SARS also showed that the spread of infectious disease can be contained when effective global institutions, such as the World Health Organization (WHO), work in close partnership with functioning national health agencies and expert technical institutions. No State could have achieved this degree of containment on its own. **To strengthen existing mechanisms for timely and effective international cooperation, I call on Member States to agree on the revision of the International Health Regulations at the World Health Assembly to be held in May 2005.** To contain the risk of future outbreaks, greater resources should also be given to the WHO Global Outbreak Alert and Response Network so that it can coordinate the response of a broad international partnership in support of national health surveillance and response systems.

Natural disasters

65. The devastating impact of the Indian Ocean tsunami has reminded us all of the vulnerability of human life to natural disasters, and also of the disproportionate effect they have on poor people. Unless more determined efforts are made to address the loss of lives, livelihoods and infrastructure, disasters will become an increasingly serious obstacle to the achievement of the Millennium Development Goals. The World Conference on Disaster Reduction, held in early 2005, adopted the Hyogo Framework for Action 2005-2015, which identifies strategic objectives and priority areas to reduce disaster risk in the next 10 years. We must proceed with its implementation.

66. The countries of the Indian Ocean region, with the help of the United Nations and others, are now taking steps to establish a regional tsunami early warning system. Let us not forget, however, the other hazards that people in all regions of the world are exposed to, including storms, floods, droughts, landslides, heat waves and volcanic eruptions. **To complement broader disaster preparedness and mitigation initiatives, I recommend the establishment of a worldwide early warning system for all natural hazards, building on existing national and regional capacity.** To assist in

its establishment, I shall be requesting the International Strategy for Disaster Reduction secretariat to coordinate a survey of existing capacities and gaps, in cooperation with all United Nations system entities concerned, and I look forward to receiving its findings and recommendations. When disasters strike, we also need improved rapid response arrangements for immediate humanitarian relief, which are considered in section V below.

Science and technology for development

67. **To help drive economic development and to enable developing countries to forge solutions to their own problems, a significantly increased global effort is required to support research and development to address the special needs of the poor in the areas of health, agriculture, natural resource and environmental management, energy and climate.** Two particular priorities should be to mount a major global initiative on research in tropical diseases and to provide additional support to the Consultative Group on International Agricultural Research (CGIAR) for research on tropical agriculture.

68. Information and communication technologies can significantly contribute to the achievement of the Millennium Development Goals. To fully utilize the potential of information and communication technology (ICT), we need to address the digital divide, including through voluntary financing mechanisms, such as the recently launched Digital Solidarity Fund.

Regional infrastructure and institutions

69. Regional infrastructure and policy cooperation are essential for supporting economic development. This is particularly so when developing countries are landlocked or small islands, both of which need special support. But other countries that may simply have small populations, or are dependent on their neighbours for transport, food, water or energy, also need assistance. International donors should support regional cooperation to deal with these problems, and developing countries should make such cooperation an integral part of their national strategies. This should cover not only economic cooperation but also mechanisms for regional political dialogue and consensus-building, such as the African Peer Review Mechanism and the New Partnership for Africa's Development (NEPAD).

Global institutions

70. The international financial institutions are essential to ensuring development around the world and successful implementation of the Millennium Development Goals. I encourage them to ensure that the country programmes they support are ambitious enough to achieve the Millennium Development Goals. In addition, these institutions and their shareholders should consider what changes they might undergo in order to better reflect the changes in the world's political economy since

1945. This should be done in the context of the Monterrey Consensus agreement to broaden and strengthen the participation of developing and transition countries in international economic decision-making and norm-setting. The Bretton Woods institutions have already taken some steps to strengthen the voice and participation of developing countries. But more significant steps are needed to overcome the widespread perception among developing countries that they are underrepresented in both bodies, which in turn tends to put their legitimacy in doubt.

Migration

71. Today, more people live outside their countries of origin than at any time in history and their numbers are expected to increase in the future. Migration offers many opportunities — to the migrants themselves, to the countries that receive younger workforce and also — notably in the form of remittance payments, which have grown spectacularly in recent years — to their countries of origin. But it also involves many complex challenges. It can contribute simultaneously to unemployment in one region or sector and to labour shortages and "brain drains" in another. If not carefully managed, it can also provoke acute social and political tensions. The impact of these trends is not yet well understood, but I believe that the report of the Global Commission on International Migration, which I shall receive later in 2005, will provide some valuable guidance. The high-level dialogue on the subject to be held by the General Assembly in 2006 will provide an important opportunity to tackle the hard questions on this issue.

F. THE IMPLEMENTATION CHALLENGE

72. The urgent task in 2005 is to implement in full the commitments already made and to render genuinely operational the framework already in place. The principles of mutual responsibility and mutual accountability that underpinned the Monterrey Consensus are sound and need to be translated into deeds. The September summit must produce a pact for action, to which all nations subscribe and on which all can be judged. The Millennium Development Goals must no longer be floating targets, referred to now and then to measure progress. They must inform, on a daily basis, national strategies and international assistance alike. Without a bold breakthrough in 2005 that lays the groundwork for a rapid progress in coming years, we will miss the targets. Let us be clear about the costs of missing this opportunity: millions of lives that could have been saved will be lost; many freedoms that could have been secured will be denied; and we shall inhabit a more dangerous and unstable world.

73. By the same token, development would be at best hindered and at worst reversed in a world riven by violent conflict or mesmerized by the fear of terrorism and weapons of mass destruction, or one in which human rights were trampled, the rule of law was disregarded and citizens' views and needs were ignored by unresponsive and

unrepresentative Governments. Progress on the issues covered in sections III and IV below, therefore, is essential to realizing the objectives set out above, just as development is itself an indispensable underpinning for longer-term security, human rights and the rule of law.

Box 4

The special needs of Africa

The problems discussed in the present report are global in nature, and solutions must be global. Yet almost all of them affect Africa disproportionately. If we are to achieve truly global solutions, we must recognize Africa's special needs, as world leaders did in the Millennium Declaration. From action to achieve the Millennium Development Goals to better collective capacity to build peace and strengthen States, the special needs of Africa lie at the heart of every part of the present report.

There have been some positive developments in Africa in the past five years. Today, more African States have democratically elected Governments than ever before and the number of military coups on the continent has declined significantly. Some long-standing conflicts, such as those in Angola and Sierra Leone, have been resolved. From Uganda to Mozambique, many individual countries are experiencing rapid and sustained economic and social recovery. And throughout the continent, ordinary people are organizing themselves and making their voices heard.

And yet much of Africa — especially south of the Sahara — continues to suffer the tragic effects of persistent violent conflict, extreme poverty and disease. Some 2.8 million refugees — and fully half of the world's 24.6 million internally displaced people — are victims of conflict and upheaval in Africa. Africa continues to lag behind the rest of the developing world in achieving the Millennium Development Goals. About three quarters of the world's AIDS deaths every year occur in Africa, with women the most affected. The high prevalence of HIV/AIDS in many African countries is both a human tragedy and a major obstacle to development. Of the 1 million or more people in the world killed by malaria each year, roughly 90 per cent are killed in sub-Saharan Africa, most of them children less than five years old. Much of sub-Saharan Africa continues to face a combination of high transport costs and small markets, low agricultural productivity, a very high disease burden and slow diffusion of technology from abroad. All these make it particularly prone to persistent poverty.

Today, African States are addressing these problems with new energy and determination. They are adopting more robust development strategies to meet the Millennium Development Goals by 2015. Africa is building a new architecture of institutions, including the African Union and the New Partnership for Africa's Development, through which to prevent, manage and resolve violent conflict, promote good governance and democracy, and create the right conditions for its economies to grow and thrive in a sustainable way.

As the Commission on Africa set up by the United Kingdom reported in March 2005, Africa's leaders and people will need special support from the rest of the world to succeed in these pioneering efforts. The international community must respond to this need. It must give tangible and sustained support to African countries and regional and subregional organizations, in a spirit of partnership and solidarity. This means ensuring follow-through on existing and needed commitments on debt relief, opening markets and providing greatly increased official development assistance. It also means contributing troops for peacekeeping operations and strengthening the capacity of African States to provide security for their citizens and to meet their needs.

III. Freedom from fear

III. Freedom from fear

74. While, in the development sphere, we suffer from weak implementation, on the security side, despite a heightened sense of threat among many, we lack even a basic consensus, and implementation, where it occurs, is all too often contested.

75. Unless we can agree on a shared assessment of these threats and a common understanding of our obligations in addressing them, the United Nations will lag in providing security to all of its Members and all the world's people. Our ability to assist those who seek freedom from fear will then be partial at best.

A. A VISION OF COLLECTIVE SECURITY

76. In November 2003, alarmed by the lack of agreement among Member States on the proper role of the United Nations in providing collective security — or even on the nature of the most compelling threats that we face — I set up the High-level Panel on Threats, Challenges and Change. The Panel delivered its report, "A more secure world: our shared responsibility" (A/59/565), in December 2004.

77. I fully embrace the broad vision that the report articulates and its case for a more comprehensive concept of collective security: one that tackles new threats and old and that addresses the security concerns of all States. I believe that this concept can bridge the gap between divergent views of security and give us the guidance we need to face today's dilemmas.

78. The threats to peace and security in the twenty-first century include not just international war and conflict but civil violence, organized crime, terrorism and weapons of mass destruction. They also include poverty, deadly infectious disease and environmental degradation, since these can have equally catastrophic consequences. All of these threats can cause death or lessen life chances on a large scale. All of them can undermine States as the basic unit of the international system.

79. Depending on wealth, geography and power, we perceive different threats as the most pressing. But the truth is we cannot afford to choose. Collective security today depends on accepting that the threats which each region of the world perceives as most urgent are in fact equally so for all.

80. In our globalized world, the threats we face are interconnected. The rich are vulnerable to the threats that attack the poor and the strong are vulnerable to the weak, as well as vice versa. A nuclear terrorist attack on the United States or Europe would have devastating effects on the whole world. But so would the appearance of a new virulent pandemic disease in a poor country with no effective health-care system.

81. On this interconnectedness of threats we must found a new security consensus, the first article of which must be that all are entitled to freedom from fear, and that

whatever threatens one threatens all. Once we understand this, we have no choice but to tackle the whole range of threats. We must respond to HIV/AIDS as robustly as we do to terrorism and to poverty as effectively as we do to proliferation. We must strive just as hard to eliminate the threat of small arms and light weapons as we do to eliminate the threat of weapons of mass destruction. Moreover, we must address all these threats preventively, acting at a sufficiently early stage with the full range of available instruments.

82.　We need to ensure that States abide by the security treaties they have signed so that all can continue to reap the benefit. More consistent monitoring, more effective implementation and, where necessary, firmer enforcement are essential if States are to have confidence in multilateral mechanisms and use them to avoid conflict.

83.　These are not theoretical issues but issues of deadly urgency. If we do not reach a consensus on them this year and start to act on it, we may not have another chance. This year, if ever, we must transform the United Nations into the effective instrument for preventing conflict that it was always meant to be by acting on several key policy and institutional priorities.

84.　We must act to ensure that catastrophic terrorism never becomes a reality. This will require a new global strategy, which begins with Member States agreeing on a definition of terrorism and including it in a comprehensive convention. It will also require all States to sign, ratify, implement and comply with comprehensive conventions against organized crime and corruption. And it will require from them a commitment to take urgent steps to prevent nuclear, chemical and biological weapons getting into the hands of terrorist groups.

85.　We must revitalize our multilateral frameworks for handling threats from nuclear, biological and chemical weapons. The threat posed by these weapons is not limited to terrorist use. The existence of multilateral instruments to promote disarmament and prevent proliferation among States has been central to the maintenance of international peace and security ever since those instruments were agreed. But they are now in danger of erosion. They must be revitalized to ensure continued progress on disarmament and to address the growing risk of a cascade of proliferation, especially in the nuclear field.

86.　We must continue to reduce the prevalence and risk of war. This requires both the emphasis on development outlined in section II above and the strengthening of tools to deliver the military and civilian support needed to prevent and end wars as well as to build a sustainable peace. Investment in prevention, peacemaking, peacekeeping and peacebuilding can save millions of lives. If only two peace agreements had been successfully implemented in the early 1990s — the Bicesse Accords in Angola and the Arusha Accords in Rwanda — we could have prevented the deaths of almost 3 million people.

B. PREVENTING CATASTROPHIC TERRORISM

Transnational terrorism

87. Terrorism is a threat to all that the United Nations stands for: respect for human rights, the rule of law, the protection of civilians, tolerance among peoples and nations, and the peaceful resolution of conflict. It is a threat that has grown more urgent in the last five years. Transnational networks of terrorist groups have global reach and make common cause to pose a universal threat. Such groups profess a desire to acquire nuclear, biological and chemical weapons and to inflict mass casualties. Even one such attack and the chain of events it might set off could change our world forever.

88. Our strategy against terrorism must be comprehensive and should be based on five pillars: it must aim at dissuading people from resorting to terrorism or supporting it; it must deny terrorists access to funds and materials; it must deter States from sponsoring terrorism; it must develop State capacity to defeat terrorism; and it must defend human rights. **I urge Member States and civil society organizations everywhere to join in that strategy.**

89. Several steps are urgently required, as described below.

90. We must convince all those who may be tempted to support terrorism that it is neither an acceptable nor an effective way to advance their cause. But the moral authority of the United Nations and its strength in condemning terrorism have been hampered by the inability of Member States to agree on a comprehensive convention that includes a definition.

91. It is time to set aside debates on so-called "State terrorism". The use of force by States is already thoroughly regulated under international law. And the right to resist occupation must be understood in its true meaning. It cannot include the right to deliberately kill or maim civilians. I endorse fully the High-level Panel's call for a definition of terrorism, which would make it clear that, in addition to actions already proscribed by existing conventions, any action constitutes terrorism if it is intended to cause death or serious bodily harm to civilians or non-combatants with the purpose of intimidating a population or compelling a Government or an international organization to do or abstain from doing any act. **I believe this proposal has clear moral force, and I strongly urge world leaders to unite behind it and to conclude a comprehensive convention on terrorism before the end of the sixtieth session of the General Assembly.**

92. It is vital that we deny terrorists access to nuclear materials. This means consolidating, securing and, when possible, eliminating hazardous materials and implementing effective export controls. While the Group of Eight Major Industrialized Countries (G8) and the Security Council have taken important steps to do this, we need to make sure that these measures are fully enforced and that they rein-

force each other. **I urge Member States to complete, without delay, an international convention for the suppression of acts of nuclear terrorism.**

93.   The threat of biological terrorism differs from that of nuclear terrorism. There will soon be thousands of laboratories around the world capable of producing designer bugs with awesome lethal potential. Our best defence against this danger lies in strengthening public health, and the recommendations to this end contained in section II above have a double merit: they would both help to address the scourge of naturally occurring infectious disease and contribute to our safety against man-made outbreaks. As we commit ourselves to strengthen local health systems — a task that will take us a generation — we must also ensure that our existing global response is adequate. The World Health Organization Global Outbreak Alert and Response Network has done an impressive job in monitoring and responding to outbreaks of deadly infectious disease, whether natural or suspicious. But it has done so on a shoestring. **I urge Member States to give it the resources it needs to do the job thoroughly, in all our interests.**

94.   Terrorists are accountable to no one. We, on the other hand, must never lose sight of our accountability to citizens all around the world. In our struggle against terrorism, we must never compromise human rights. When we do so we facilitate achievement of one of the terrorists' objectives. By ceding the moral high ground we provoke tension, hatred and mistrust of Governments among precisely those parts of the population where terrorists find recruits. **I urge Member States to create a special rapporteur who would report to the Commission on Human Rights on the compatibility of counter-terrorism measures with international human rights laws.**

Organized crime

95.   The threat of terrorism is closely linked to that of organized crime, which is growing and affects the security of all States. Organized crime contributes to State weakness, impedes economic growth, fuels many civil wars, regularly undermines United Nations peacebuilding efforts and provides financing mechanisms to terrorist groups. Organized criminal groups are also heavily involved in the illegal smuggling of migrants and trafficking in firearms.

96.   In recent years, the United Nations has made important progress in building a framework of international standards and norms for the fight against organized crime and corruption, with the adoption or entry into force of several major conventions and protocols. However, many of the States parties to these treaties have not implemented them adequately, sometimes because they genuinely lack the capacity to do so. **All States should both ratify and implement these conventions, while helping each other to strengthen their domestic criminal justice and rule-of-law systems. And Member States should give adequate resources to the United**

Nations Office on Drugs and Crime for its key role in overseeing implementation of the conventions.

C. NUCLEAR, BIOLOGICAL AND CHEMICAL WEAPONS

97. Multilateral efforts to bridle the dangers of nuclear technology while harnessing its promise are nearly as old as the United Nations itself. The Treaty on the Non-Proliferation of Nuclear Weapons,[12] 35 years old this month, has proved indispensable: it has not only diminished nuclear peril but also demonstrated the value of multilateral agreements in safeguarding international peace and security. But today, the Treaty has suffered the first withdrawal of a party to the Treaty and faces a crisis of confidence and compliance born of a growing strain on verification and enforcement. The Conference on Disarmament, for its part, faces a crisis of relevance resulting in part from dysfunctional decision-making procedures and the paralysis that accompanies them.

98. Progress in both disarmament and non-proliferation is essential and neither should be held hostage to the other. Recent moves towards disarmament by the nuclear-weapon States should be recognized. Bilateral agreements, including the 2002 Strategic Offensive Reductions Treaty signed by the United States and the Russian Federation, have led to the dismantlement of thousands of nuclear weapons, accompanied by commitments to further sharp reductions in stockpiles. **However, the unique status of nuclear-weapon States also entails a unique responsibility, and they must do more, including but not limited to further reductions in their arsenals of non-strategic nuclear weapons and pursuing arms control agreements that entail not just dismantlement but irreversibility. They should also reaffirm their commitment to negative security assurances. Swift negotiation of a fissile material cut-off treaty is essential. The moratorium on nuclear test explosions must also be upheld until we can achieve the entry into force of the Comprehensive Nuclear-Test-Ban Treaty. I strongly encourage States parties to the Treaty on the Non-Proliferation of Nuclear Weapons to endorse these measures at the 2005 Review Conference.**

99. The spread of nuclear technology has exacerbated a long-standing tension within the nuclear regime, arising from the simple fact that the technology required for civilian nuclear fuel can also be used to develop nuclear weapons. Measures to mitigate this tension must confront the dangers of nuclear proliferation but must also take into account the important environmental, energy, economic and research applications of nuclear technology. **First, the verification authority of the International Atomic Energy Agency (IAEA) must be strengthened through universal adoption of the Model Additional Protocol. Second, while the access of non-nuclear-weapon States to the benefits of nuclear technology should not be curtailed, we should focus on creating incentives for States to voluntarily forgo the development of domestic uranium enrichment and plutonium separation capacities, while**

guaranteeing their supply of the fuel necessary to develop peaceful uses. One option is an arrangement in which IAEA would act as a guarantor for the supply of fissile material to civilian nuclear users at market rates.

100.   While the Treaty on the Non-Proliferation of Nuclear Weapons remains the foundation of the non-proliferation regime, we should welcome recent efforts to supplement it. These include Security Council resolution 1540 (2004), designed to prevent non-State actors from gaining access to nuclear, chemical and biological weapons, technology and materials, and their means of delivery; and the voluntary Proliferation Security Initiative, under which more and more States are cooperating to prevent illicit trafficking in nuclear, biological and chemical weapons.

101.   The availability of ballistic missiles with extended range and greater accuracy is of growing concern to many States, as is the spread of shoulder-fired missiles which could be used by terrorists. **Member States should adopt effective national export controls covering missiles and other means of delivery for nuclear, biological and chemical weapons, rockets and shoulder-fired missiles, as well as a ban on transferring any of them to non-State actors.** The Security Council should also consider adopting a resolution aimed at making it harder for terrorists to acquire or use shoulder-fired missiles.

102.   Where progress has been made, it should be consolidated. The 1997 Convention on the Prohibition of the Development, Production, Stockpiling and Use of Chemical Weapons and on Their Destruction[13] calls for the complete elimination and destruction of chemical weapons by all States parties, thus offering a historic opportunity to complete a task begun more than a century ago. **States parties to the Convention on Chemical Weapons should recommit themselves to achieving the scheduled destruction of declared chemical weapons stockpiles. I call upon all States to accede immediately to the Convention.**

103.   The 1975 Convention on the Prohibition of the Development, Production and Stockpiling of Bacteriological (Biological) and Toxin Weapons and on Their Destruction[14] has enjoyed a remarkable degree of support and adherence, and has been strengthened further through recent annual meetings. **States parties should consolidate the results of these meetings at the 2006 Review Conference and commit themselves to further measures to strengthen the Biological and Toxin Weapons Convention. I also call upon all States to accede immediately to the Convention and to increase the transparency of bio-defence programmes.**

104.   Further efforts are needed to bolster the biological security regime. The capability of the Secretary-General to investigate suspected use of biological agents, as authorized by the General Assembly in its resolution 42/37, should be strengthened to incorporate the latest technology and expertise; and the Security Council should make use of that capability, consistent with Security Council resolution 620 (1988).

105. Indeed, the Security Council must be better informed on all matters relevant to nuclear, chemical and biological threats. I encourage the Council to regularly invite the Director General of IAEA and the Director-General of the Organization for the Prohibition of Chemical Weapons to brief the Council on the status of safeguards and verification processes. And I myself stand ready, in consultation with the Director-General of the World Health Organization, to use my powers under Article 99 of the Charter of the United Nations to call to the attention of the Security Council any overwhelming outbreak of infectious disease that threatens international peace and security.

D. Reducing the risk and prevalence of war

106. No task is more fundamental to the United Nations than the prevention and resolution of deadly conflict. Prevention, in particular, must be central to all our efforts, from combating poverty and promoting sustainable development; through strengthening national capacities to manage conflict, promoting democracy and the rule of law, and curbing the flow of small arms and light weapons; to directing preventive operational activities, such as the use of good offices, Security Council missions and preventive deployments.

107. Member States must ensure that the United Nations has the right structure and sufficient resources to perform these vital tasks.

Mediation

108. Although it is difficult to demonstrate, the United Nations has almost certainly prevented many wars by using the Secretary-General's "good offices" to help resolve conflicts peacefully. And over the past 15 years, more civil wars have ended through mediation than in the previous two centuries, in large part because the United Nations provided leadership, opportunities for negotiation, strategic coordination and the resources to implement peace agreements. But we could undoubtedly save many more lives if we had the capacity and personnel to do so. **I urge Member States to allocate additional resources to the Secretary-General for his good offices function.**

Sanctions

109. Sanctions are a vital tool at the disposal of the Security Council for dealing preventively with threats to international peace and security. They constitute a necessary middle ground between war and words. In some cases, sanctions can help to produce agreements. In others, they can be combined with military pressure to weaken and isolate rebel groups or States that are in flagrant violation of Security Council resolutions.

110. The use of financial, diplomatic, arms, aviation, travel and commodity sanctions to target belligerents, in particular the individuals most directly responsible for reprehensible policies, will continue to be a vital tool in the United Nations arsenal. **All Security Council sanctions should be effectively implemented and enforced by strengthening State capacity to implement sanctions, establishing well-resourced monitoring mechanisms and mitigating humanitarian consequences.** Given the difficult environments in which sanctions are often used and the lessons learned in recent years, future sanctions regimes must also be structured carefully so as to minimize the suffering caused to innocent third parties — including the civilian populations of targeted States — and to protect the integrity of the programmes and institutions involved.

Peacekeeping

111. Over the decades, the United Nations has done a great deal to stabilize zones of conflict, and in the last 15 years or so also to help countries emerge from conflict, by deploying peacekeeping forces. Since the issuance of the report of the Panel on United Nations Peace Operations (A/55/305-S/2000/809, annex), which led to important reforms in the management of our peacekeeping operations, the renewed confidence of Member States in United Nations peacekeeping has led to a surge in demand, with the result that the United Nations now has more missions on the ground than ever before. The majority of these are in Africa, where — I regret to say — developed countries are increasingly reluctant to contribute troops. As a result, our capacity is severely stretched.

112. **I appeal to Member States to do more to ensure that the United Nations has effective capacities for peacekeeping, commensurate with the demands that they place upon it.** In particular, I urge them to improve our deployment options by creating strategic reserves that can be deployed rapidly, within the framework of United Nations arrangements. United Nations capacity should not be developed in competition with the admirable efforts now being made by many regional organizations but in cooperation with them. Decisions by the European Union to create standby battle groups, for instance, and by the African Union to create African reserve capacities, are a very valuable complement to our own efforts. **Indeed, I believe the time is now ripe for a decisive move forward: the establishment of an interlocking system of peacekeeping capacities that will enable the United Nations to work with relevant regional organizations in predictable and reliable partnerships.**

113. Since the rule of law is an essential element of lasting peace, United Nations peacekeepers and peacebuilders have a solemn responsibility to respect the law themselves, and especially to respect the rights of the people whom it is their mission to help. In the light of recent allegations of misconduct by United Nations administrators and peacekeepers, the United Nations system should reaffirm its commitment to respect, adhere to and implement international law, fundamental

human rights and the basic standards of due process. I will work to strengthen the internal capacity of the United Nations to exercise oversight of peacekeeping operations, and I remind Member States of their obligation to prosecute any members of their national contingents who commit crimes or offences in the States where they are deployed. **I am especially troubled by instances in which United Nations peacekeepers are alleged to have sexually exploited minors and other vulnerable people, and I have enacted a policy of "zero tolerance" towards such offences that applies to all personnel engaged in United Nations operations. I strongly encourage Member States to do the same with respect to their national contingents.**

Peacebuilding

114. Our record of success in mediating and implementing peace agreements is sadly blemished by some devastating failures. Indeed, several of the most violent and tragic episodes of the 1990s occurred after the negotiation of peace agreements — for instance in Angola in 1993 and in Rwanda in 1994. Roughly half of all countries that emerge from war lapse back into violence within five years. These two points drive home the message: if we are going to prevent conflict we must ensure that peace agreements are implemented in a sustained and sustainable manner. Yet at this very point there is a gaping hole in the United Nations institutional machinery: no part of the United Nations system effectively addresses the challenge of helping countries with the transition from war to lasting peace. **I therefore propose to Member States that they create an intergovernmental Peacebuilding Commission, as well as a Peacebuilding Support Office within the United Nations Secretariat, to achieve this end.**

115. A Peacebuilding Commission could perform the following functions: in the immediate aftermath of war, improve United Nations planning for sustained recovery, focusing on early efforts to establish the necessary institutions; help to ensure predictable financing for early recovery activities, in part by providing an overview of assessed, voluntary and standing funding mechanisms; improve the coordination of the many post-conflict activities of the United Nations funds, programmes and agencies; provide a forum in which the United Nations, major bilateral donors, troop contributors, relevant regional actors and organizations, the international financial institutions and the national or transitional Government of the country concerned can share information about their respective post-conflict recovery strategies, in the interests of greater coherence; periodically review progress towards medium-term recovery goals; and extend the period of political attention to post-conflict recovery. I do not believe that such a body should have an early warning or monitoring function, but it would be valuable if Member States could at any stage make use of the Peacebuilding Commission's advice and could request assistance from a standing fund for peacebuilding to build their domestic institutions for reducing conflict, including through strengthening the rule-of-law institutions.

116. I believe that such a body would best combine efficiency with legitimacy if it were to report to the Security Council and the Economic and Social Council in sequence, depending on the phase of the conflict. Simultaneous reporting lines should be avoided because they will create duplication and confusion.

117. The Peacebuilding Commission would be most effective if its core membership comprised a subset of Security Council members, a similar number of Economic and Social Council members, leading troop contributors and the major donors to a standing fund for peacebuilding. In its country-specific operations, the Peacebuilding Commission should involve the national or transitional authorities, relevant regional actors and organizations, troop contributors, where applicable, and the major donors to the specific country.

118. The participation of international financial institutions is vital. I have started discussions with them to determine how best they can be involved, with due respect for their mandates and governing arrangements.

119. Once these discussions are completed, in advance of September 2005, I will present Member States a more fully developed proposal for their consideration.

Small arms, light weapons and landmines

120. The accumulation and proliferation of small arms and light weapons continue to be a serious threat to peace, stability and sustainable development. Since the adoption in 2001 of the Programme of Action to Prevent, Combat and Eradicate the Illicit Trade in Small Arms and Light Weapons in All Its Aspects,[15] awareness of the problem has grown and there have been various initiatives to tackle it. We must now begin to make a real difference by ensuring better enforcement of arms embargoes, strengthening programmes for the disarmament of ex-combatants and negotiating a legally binding international instrument to regulate the marking and tracing of small arms and light weapons, as well as one to prevent, combat and eradicate illicit brokering. **I urge Member States to agree on an instrument to regulate marking and tracing no later than next year's Review Conference on the Programme of Action, and to expedite negotiations on an instrument on illicit brokering.**

121. We must also continue our work to remove the scourge of landmines, which — along with other explosive remnants of war — still kill and maim innocent people in nearly half the world's countries and hold back entire communities from working their way out of poverty. The Convention on the Prohibition of the Use, Stockpiling, Production and Transfer of Anti-Personnel Mines and on Their Destruction,[16] supplemented by Amended Protocol II[17] to the Convention on Prohibitions or Restrictions on the Use of Certain Conventional Weapons Which May Be Deemed to Be Excessively Injurious or to Have Indiscriminate Effects,[18] now has 144 States parties and has made a real difference on the ground. Transfers of mines have virtually halted, large tracts of previously mined lands have been cleared and more than

31 million stockpiled mines have been destroyed. Yet not all States parties to the Convention have fully implemented it and there are vast stockpiles of mines in the arsenals of States that remain outside it. **I therefore urge States parties to implement their obligations in full, and call on those States that have not yet done so to accede to both the Convention and the Protocol at the earliest possible moment.**

E. Use of force

122. Finally, an essential part of the consensus we seek must be agreement on when and how force can be used to defend international peace and security. In recent years, this issue has deeply divided Member States. They have disagreed about whether States have the right to use military force pre-emptively, to defend themselves against imminent threats; whether they have the right to use it preventively to defend themselves against latent or non-imminent threats; and whether they have the right — or perhaps the obligation — to use it protectively to rescue the citizens of other States from genocide or comparable crimes.

123. Agreement must be reached on these questions if the United Nations is to be — as it was intended to be — a forum for resolving differences rather than a mere stage for acting them out. And yet I believe the Charter of our Organization, as it stands, offers a good basis for the understanding that we need.

124. Imminent threats are fully covered by Article 51, which safeguards the inherent right of sovereign States to defend themselves against armed attack. Lawyers have long recognized that this covers an imminent attack as well as one that has already happened.

125. Where threats are not imminent but latent, the Charter gives full authority to the Security Council to use military force, including preventively, to preserve international peace and security. As to genocide, ethnic cleansing and other such crimes against humanity, are they not also threats to international peace and security, against which humanity should be able to look to the Security Council for protection?

126. The task is not to find alternatives to the Security Council as a source of authority but to make it work better. When considering whether to authorize or endorse the use of military force, the Council should come to a common view on how to weigh the seriousness of the threat; the proper purpose of the proposed military action; whether means short of the use of force might plausibly succeed in stopping the threat; whether the military option is proportional to the threat at hand; and whether there is a reasonable chance of success. By undertaking to make the case for military action in this way, the Council would add transparency to its deliberations and make its decisions more likely to be respected, by both Governments and world public opinion. **I therefore recommend that the Security Council adopt a resolution setting out these principles and expressing its intention to be guided by them when deciding whether to authorize or mandate the use of force.**

IV. Freedom to live in dignity

IV. Freedom to live in dignity

127. In the Millennium Declaration, Member States stated that they would spare no effort to promote democracy and strengthen the rule of law, as well as respect for all internationally recognized human rights and fundamental freedoms. In so doing, they recognized that while freedom from want and fear are essential they are not enough. All human beings have the right to be treated with dignity and respect.

128. The protection and promotion of the universal values of the rule of law, human rights and democracy are ends in themselves. They are also essential for a world of justice, opportunity and stability. No security agenda and no drive for development will be successful unless they are based on the sure foundation of respect for human dignity.

129. When it comes to laws on the books, no generation has inherited the riches that we have. We are blessed with what amounts to an international bill of human rights, among which are impressive norms to protect the weakest among us, including victims of conflict and persecution. We also enjoy a set of international rules on everything from trade to the law of the sea, from terrorism to the environment and from small arms to weapons of mass destruction. Through hard experience, we have become more conscious of the need to build human rights and rule-of-law provisions into peace agreements and ensure that they are implemented. And even harder experience has led us to grapple with the fact that no legal principle — not even sovereignty — should ever be allowed to shield genocide, crimes against humanity and mass human suffering.

130. But without implementation, our declarations ring hollow. Without action, our promises are meaningless. Villagers huddling in fear at the sound of government bombing raids or the appearance of murderous militias on the horizon find no solace in the unimplemented words of the Geneva Conventions, to say nothing of the international community's solemn promises of "never again" when reflecting on the horrors of Rwanda a decade ago. Treaties prohibiting torture are cold comfort to prisoners abused by their captors, particularly if the international human rights machinery enables those responsible to hide behind friends in high places. A war-weary population infused with new hope after the signing of a peace agreement quickly reverts to despair when, instead of seeing tangible progress towards a Government under the rule of law, it sees warlords and gang leaders take power and become laws unto themselves. And solemn commitments to strengthen democracy at home, which all States made in the Millennium Declaration, remain empty words to those who have never voted for their rulers and who see no sign that things are changing.

131. To advance a vision of larger freedom, the United Nations and its Member States must strengthen the normative framework that has been so impressively advanced

over the last six decades. Even more important, we must take concrete steps to reduce selective application, arbitrary enforcement and breach without consequence. Those steps would give new life to the commitments made in the Millennium Declaration.

132. Accordingly, I believe that decisions should be made in 2005 to help strengthen the rule of law internationally and nationally, enhance the stature and structure of the human rights machinery of the United Nations and more directly support efforts to institute and deepen democracy in nations around the globe. We must also move towards embracing and acting on the "responsibility to protect" potential or actual victims of massive atrocities. The time has come for Governments to be held to account, both to their citizens and to each other, for respect of the dignity of the individual, to which they too often pay only lip service. We must move from an era of legislation to an era of implementation. Our declared principles and our common interests demand no less.

A. RULE OF LAW

133. I strongly believe that every nation that proclaims the rule of law at home must respect it abroad and that every nation that insists on it abroad must enforce it at home. Indeed, the Millennium Declaration reaffirmed the commitment of all nations to the rule of law as the all-important framework for advancing human security and prosperity. Yet in many places, Governments and individuals continue to violate the rule of law, often without consequences for them but with deadly consequences for the weak and the vulnerable. In other instances, those who make no pretence of being bound by the rule of law, such as armed groups and terrorists, are able to flout it because our peacemaking institutions and compliance mechanisms are weak. The rule of law as a mere concept is not enough. New laws must be put into place, old ones must be put into practice and our institutions must be better equipped to strengthen the rule of law.

134. Nowhere is the gap between rhetoric and reality — between declarations and deeds — so stark and so deadly as in the field of international humanitarian law. It cannot be right, when the international community is faced with genocide or massive human rights abuses, for the United Nations to stand by and let them unfold to the end, with disastrous consequences for many thousands of innocent people. I have drawn Member States' attention to this issue over many years. On the occasion of the tenth anniversary of the Rwandan genocide, I presented a five-point action plan to prevent genocide. The plan underscored the need for action to prevent armed conflict, effective measures to protect civilians, judicial steps to fight impunity, early warning through a Special Adviser on the Prevention of Genocide, and swift and decisive action when genocide is happening or about to happen. Much more, how-

ever, needs to be done to prevent atrocities and to ensure that the international community acts promptly when faced with massive violations.

135. The International Commission on Intervention and State Sovereignty and more recently the High-level Panel on Threats, Challenges and Change, with its 16 members from all around the world, endorsed what they described as an "emerging norm that there is a collective responsibility to protect" (see A/59/565, para. 203). While I am well aware of the sensitivities involved in this issue, I strongly agree with this approach. **I believe that we must embrace the responsibility to protect, and, when necessary, we must act on it.** This responsibility lies, first and foremost, with each individual State, whose primary raison d'être and duty is to protect its population. But if national authorities are unable or unwilling to protect their citizens, then the responsibility shifts to the international community to use diplomatic, humanitarian and other methods to help protect the human rights and well-being of civilian populations. When such methods appear insufficient, the Security Council may out of necessity decide to take action under the Charter of the United Nations, including enforcement action, if so required. In this case, as in others, it should follow the principles set out in section III above.

136. Support for the rule of law must be strengthened by universal participation in multilateral conventions. At present, many States remain outside the multilateral conventional framework, in some cases preventing important conventions from entering into force. Five years ago, I provided special facilities for States to sign or ratify treaties of which I am the Depositary. This proved a major success and treaty events have been held annually ever since. This year's event will focus on 31 multilateral treaties to help us respond to global challenges, with emphasis on human rights, refugees, terrorism, organized crime and the law of the sea. **I urge leaders especially to ratify and implement all treaties relating to the protection of civilians.**

137. Effective national legal and judicial institutions are essential to the success of all our efforts to help societies emerge from a violent past. Yet the United Nations, other international organizations and member Governments remain ill equipped to provide support for such institutions. As I outlined in my report on the rule of law and transitional justice in conflict and post-conflict societies (S/2004/616), we lack appropriate assessment and planning capacities, both in the field and at Headquarters. As a result, assistance is often piecemeal, slow and ill suited to the ultimate goal. To help the United Nations realize its potential in this area, **I intend to create a dedicated Rule of Law Assistance Unit, drawing heavily on existing staff within the United Nations system, in the proposed Peacebuilding Support Office (see sect. V below) to assist national efforts to re-establish the rule of law in conflict and post-conflict societies.**

138. Justice is a vital component of the rule of law. Enormous progress has been made with the establishment of the International Criminal Court, the continuing work of

the two ad hoc tribunals for the former Yugoslavia and Rwanda, and the creation of a mixed tribunal in Sierra Leone and hopefully soon in Cambodia as well. Other important initiatives include commissions of experts and inquiry, such as those set up for Darfur, Timor-Leste and Côte d'Ivoire. Yet impunity continues to overshadow advances made in international humanitarian law, with tragic consequences in the form of flagrant and widespread human rights abuses continuing to this day. To increase avenues of redress for the victims of atrocities and deter further horrors, **I encourage Member States to cooperate fully with the International Criminal Court and other international or mixed war crimes tribunals, and to surrender accused persons to them upon request.**

139. The International Court of Justice lies at the centre of the international system for adjudicating disputes among States. In recent years, the Court's docket has grown significantly and a number of disputes have been settled, but resources remain scarce. **There is a need to consider means to strengthen the work of the Court.** I urge those States that have not yet done so to consider recognizing the compulsory jurisdiction of the Court — generally if possible or, failing that, at least in specific situations. I also urge all parties to bear in mind, and make greater use of, the Court's advisory powers. Measures should also be taken, with the cooperation of litigating States, to improve the Court's working methods and reduce the length of its proceedings.

B. HUMAN RIGHTS

140. Human rights are as fundamental to the poor as to the rich, and their protection is as important to the security and prosperity of the developed world as it is to that of the developing world. It would be a mistake to treat human rights as though there were a trade-off to be made between human rights and such goals as security or development. We only weaken our hand in fighting the horrors of extreme poverty or terrorism if, in our efforts to do so, we deny the very human rights that these scourges take away from citizens. Strategies based on the protection of human rights are vital for both our moral standing and the practical effectiveness of our actions.

141. Since its establishment, the United Nations has committed itself to striving for a world of peace and justice grounded in universal respect for human rights — a mission reaffirmed five years ago by the Millennium Declaration. But the system for protecting human rights at the international level is today under considerable strain. Change is needed if the United Nations is to sustain long-term, high-level engagement on human rights issues, across the range of the Organization's work.

142. Important change is already under way. Since the Millennium Declaration, the United Nations human rights machinery has expanded its protection work, technical assistance and support for national human rights institutions, so that

international human rights standards are now better implemented in many countries. Last year, I launched "Action 2", a global programme designed to equip United Nations inter-agency country teams to work with Member States, at their request, to bolster their national human rights promotion and protection systems. **This programme urgently needs more resources and staff, including a stronger capacity to train country teams within the Office of the United Nations High Commissioner for Human Rights.**

143. But technical assistance and long-term institution-building are of little or no value where the basic principle of protection is being actively violated. A greater human rights field presence during times of crisis would provide timely information to United Nations bodies and, when necessary, draw urgent attention to situations requiring action.

144. The increasing frequency of the Security Council's invitations to the High Commissioner to brief it on specific situations shows that there is now a greater awareness of the need to take human rights into account in resolutions on peace and security. **The High Commissioner must play a more active role in the deliberations of the Security Council and of the proposed Peacebuilding Commission, with emphasis on the implementation of relevant provisions in Security Council resolutions.** Indeed, human rights must be incorporated into decision-making and discussion throughout the work of the Organization. The concept of "mainstreaming" human rights has gained greater attention in recent years, but it has still not been adequately reflected in key policy and resource decisions.

145. These observations all point to the need to strengthen the Office of the High Commissioner for Human Rights. While the role of the High Commissioner has expanded in the areas of crisis response, national human rights capacity-building, support for the Millennium Development Goals and conflict prevention, her Office remains woefully ill equipped to respond to the broad range of human rights challenges facing the international community. **Member States' proclaimed commitment to human rights must be matched by resources to strengthen the Office's ability to discharge its vital mandate. I have asked the High Commissioner to submit a plan of action within 60 days.**

146. The High Commissioner and her Office need to be involved in the whole spectrum of United Nations activities. But this can only work if the intergovernmental foundations of our human rights machinery are strong. In section V below, therefore, I shall make a proposal to transform the body which should be the central pillar of the United Nations human rights system — the Commission on Human Rights.

147. But the human rights treaty bodies, too, need to be much more effective and more responsive to violations of the rights that they are mandated to uphold. The treaty body system remains little known; is compromised by the failure of many States to report on time if at all, as well as the duplication of reporting requirements; and is

weakened further by poor implementation of recommendations. **Harmonized guidelines on reporting to all treaty bodies should be finalized and implemented so that these bodies can function as a unified system.**

C. DEMOCRACY

148. The Universal Declaration of Human Rights,[19] adopted by the General Assembly in 1948, enunciated the essentials of democracy. Ever since its adoption, it has inspired constitution-making in every corner of the world, and it has contributed greatly to the eventual global acceptance of democracy as a universal value. The right to choose how they are ruled, and who rules them, must be the birthright of all people, and its universal achievement must be a central objective of an organization devoted to the cause of larger freedom.

149. In the Millennium Declaration, every Member State pledged to strengthen its capacity to implement the principles and practices of democracy. That same year, the General Assembly adopted a resolution on promoting and consolidating democracy.[20] More than 100 countries have now signed the Warsaw Declaration of the Community of Democracies (see A/55/328, annex I), and in 2002 that Community endorsed the Seoul Plan of Action (see A/57/618, annex I), which listed the essential elements of representative democracy and set forth a range of measures to promote it. Regional organizations in many parts of the world have made democracy promotion a core component of their work, and the emergence of a strong community of global and regional civil society organizations that promote democratic governance is also encouraging — all of which reinforces the principle that democracy does not belong to any country or region but is a universal right.

150. However, commitments must be matched by performance and protecting democracy requires vigilance. Threats to democracy have by no means ceased to exist. As we have seen time and again, the transition to democracy is delicate and difficult and can suffer severe setbacks. The United Nations assists Member States by supporting emerging democracies with legal, technical and financial assistance and advice. For example, the United Nations has given concrete support for elections in more and more countries, often at decisive moments in their history — more than 20 in the last year alone, including Afghanistan, Palestine, Iraq and Burundi. Similarly, the Organization's work to improve governance throughout the developing world and to rebuild the rule of law and State institutions in war-torn countries is vital to ensuring that democracy takes root and endures.

151. The United Nations does more than any other single organization to promote and strengthen democratic institutions and practices around the world, but this fact is little known. The impact of our work is reduced by the way we disperse it among different parts of our bureaucracy. It is time to join up the dots. But there are significant gaps in our capacity in several critical areas. The Organization as a whole

needs to be better coordinated and should mobilize resources more effectively. The United Nations should not restrict its role to norm-setting but should expand its help to its members to further broaden and deepen democratic trends throughout the world. **To that end, I support the creation of a democracy fund at the United Nations to provide assistance to countries seeking to establish or strengthen their democracy. Furthermore, I intend to ensure that our activities in this area are more closely coordinated by establishing a more explicit link between the democratic governance work of the United Nations Development Programme and the Electoral Assistance Division of the Department of Political Affairs.**

152. In sections II to IV, I have outlined the interconnected challenges of advancing the cause of larger freedom in the new century. I have also indicated what I believe to be the essential elements of our collective response, including many areas where I believe the United Nations should be better equipped to make its proper contribution. In section V below, I shall focus in some detail on the specific reforms that I believe are needed if our Organization is to play its due part in shaping and implementing such a collective response across the whole range of global issues.

V. Strengthening the United Nations

V. Strengthening the United Nations

153. In the present report, I have argued that the principles and purposes of the United Nations, as set out in the Charter, remain as valid and relevant today as they were in 1945, and that the present moment is a precious opportunity to put them into practice. But while purposes should be firm and principles constant, practice and organization need to move with the times. If the United Nations is to be a useful instrument for its Member States and for the world's peoples, in responding to the challenges described in sections II to IV above it must be fully adapted to the needs and circumstances of the twenty-first century. It must be open not only to States but also to civil society, which at both the national and international levels plays an increasingly important role in world affairs. Its strength must be drawn from the breadth of its partnerships and from its ability to bring those partners into effective coalitions for change across the whole spectrum of issues on which action is required to advance the cause of larger freedom.

154. Clearly our Organization, as an organization, was built for a different era. Equally clearly, not all our current practices are adapted to the needs of today. That is why Heads of State and Government, in the Millennium Declaration, recognized the need to strengthen the United Nations to make it a more effective instrument for pursuing their priorities.

155. Indeed, ever since I took office as Secretary-General in 1997, one of my main priorities has been to reform the internal structures and culture of the United Nations to make the Organization more useful to its Member States and to the world's peoples. And much has been achieved. Today, the Organization's structures are more streamlined, its working methods more effective and its various programmes better coordinated, and it has developed working partnerships in many areas with civil society and the private sector. In the economic and social spheres, the Millennium Development Goals now serve as a common policy framework for the entire United Nations system, and indeed for the broader international development community. United Nations peacekeeping missions today are much better designed than they used to be, and have a more integrated understanding of the many different tasks involved in preventing a recurrence of fighting and laying the foundations of lasting peace. And we have built strategic partnerships with a wide range of non-State actors who have an important contribution to make to global security, prosperity and freedom.

156. But many more changes are needed. As things stand now, different governance structures for the many parts of the system, overlapping mandates and mandates that reflect earlier rather than current priorities all combine to hobble our effectiveness. It is essential to give managers real authority so that they can fully align the

system's activities with the goals endorsed by Member States — which I hope will be those outlined in the present report. We must also do more to professionalize the Secretariat and to hold its staff and management more rigorously accountable for their performance. And we need to ensure greater coherence, both among the various United Nations representatives and activities in each country and in the wider United Nations system, particularly in the economic and social fields.

157. But reform, if it is to be effective, cannot be confined to the executive branch. It is time to breathe new life also into the intergovernmental organs of the United Nations.

A. GENERAL ASSEMBLY

158. As the Millennium Declaration reaffirmed, the General Assembly has a central position as the chief deliberative, policy-making and representative organ of the United Nations. In particular, it has the authority to consider and approve the budget and it elects the members of the other deliberative bodies, including the Security Council. Member States are therefore rightly concerned about the decline in the Assembly's prestige and its diminishing contribution to the Organization's activities. This decline must be reversed, and that will only happen if the Assembly becomes more effective.

159. In recent years, the number of General Assembly resolutions approved by consensus has increased steadily. That would be good if it reflected a genuine unity of purpose among Member States in responding to global challenges. But unfortunately, consensus (often interpreted as requiring unanimity) has become an end in itself. It is sought first within each regional group and then at the level of the whole. This has not proved an effective way of reconciling the interests of Member States. Rather, it prompts the Assembly to retreat into generalities, abandoning any serious effort to take action. Such real debates as there are tend to focus on process rather than substance and many so-called decisions simply reflect the lowest common denominator of widely different opinions.

160. Member States agree, as they have for years, that the Assembly needs to streamline its procedures and structures so as to improve the deliberative process and make it more effective. Many modest steps have been taken. Now, new proposals to "revitalize" the Assembly have been put forward by a wide range of Member States. **The General Assembly should now take bold measures to rationalize its work and speed up the deliberative process, notably by streamlining its agenda, its committee structure and its procedures for holding plenary debates and requesting reports, and by strengthening the role and authority of its President.**

161. At present, the General Assembly addresses a broad agenda covering a wide range of often overlapping issues. **It should give focus to its substantive agenda by concentrating on addressing the major substantive issues of the day, such as international migration and the long-debated comprehensive convention on terrorism.**

162. It should also engage much more actively with civil society — reflecting the fact that, after a decade of rapidly increasing interaction, civil society is now involved in most United Nations activities. Indeed, the goals of the United Nations can only be achieved if civil society and Governments are fully engaged. The Panel of Eminent Persons on United Nations–Civil Society Relations, which I appointed in 2003, made many useful recommendations for improving our work with civil society, and I have commended its report (see A/58/817 and Corr.1) to the General Assembly together with my views. **The General Assembly should act on these recommendations and establish mechanisms enabling it to engage fully and systematically with civil society.**

163. The Assembly also needs to review its committee structure, the way committees function, the oversight it provides to them and their outputs. The General Assembly needs a mechanism to review the decisions of its committees so as to avoid overloading the Organization with unfunded mandates and continuing the current problem of micromanagement of the budget and the allocation of posts within the Secretariat. If the General Assembly cannot solve these problems, it will not have the focus and flexibility it needs to serve its members effectively.

164. It should be clear that none of this will happen unless Member States take a serious interest in the Assembly at the highest level and insist that their representatives engage in its debates with a view to achieving real and positive results. If they fail to do this the Assembly's performance will continue to disappoint them and they should not be surprised.

B. The Councils

165. Its founders endowed the United Nations with three Councils, each having major responsibilities in its own area: the Security Council, the Economic and Social Council and the Trusteeship Council. Over time, the division of responsibilities between them has become less and less balanced: the Security Council has increasingly asserted its authority and, especially since the end of the cold war, has enjoyed greater unity of purpose among its permanent members but has seen that authority questioned on the grounds that its composition is anachronistic or insufficiently representative; the Economic and Social Council has been too often relegated to the margins of global economic and social governance; and the Trusteeship Council, having successfully carried out its functions, is now reduced to a purely formal existence.

166. I believe we need to restore the balance, with three Councils covering, respectively, (a) international peace and security, (b) economic and social issues, and (c) human rights, the promotion of which has been one of the purposes of the Organization from its beginnings but now clearly requires more effective operational structures. These Councils together should have the task of driving forward the agenda that

emerges from summit and other conferences of Member States, and should be the global forms in which the issues of security, development and justice can be properly addressed. The first two Councils, of course, already exist but need to be strengthened. The third requires a far-reaching overhaul and upgrading of our existing human rights machinery.

Security Council

167. By adhering to the Charter of the United Nations, all Member States recognize that the Security Council has the primary responsibility for the maintenance of international peace and security and agree to be bound by its decisions. It is therefore of vital importance, not only to the Organization but to the world, that the Council should be equipped to carry out this responsibility and that its decisions should command worldwide respect.

168. In the Millennium Declaration, all States resolved to intensify their efforts "to achieve a comprehensive reform of the Security Council in all its aspects" (see General Assembly resolution 55/2, para. 30). This reflected the view, long held by the majority, that a change in the Council's composition is needed to make it more broadly representative of the international community as a whole, as well as of the geopolitical realities of today, and thereby more legitimate in the eyes of the world. Its working methods also need to be made more efficient and transparent. The Council must be not only more representative but also more able and willing to take action when action is needed. Reconciling these two imperatives is the hard test that any reform proposal must pass.

169. Two years ago, I declared that in my view no reform of the United Nations would be complete without reform of the Security Council. That is still my belief. The Security Council must be broadly representative of the realities of power in today's world. I therefore support the position set out in the report of the High-level Panel on Threats, Challenges and Change (A/59/565) concerning the reforms of the Security Council, namely:

    (a) They should, in honouring Article 23 of the Charter, increase the involvement in decision-making of those who contribute most to the United Nations financially, militarily and diplomatically, specifically in terms of contributions to United Nations assessed budgets, participation in mandated peace operations, contributions to voluntary activities of the United Nations in the areas of security and development, and diplomatic activities in support of United Nations objectives and mandates. Among developed countries, achieving or making substantial progress towards the internationally agreed level of 0.7 per cent of GNP for ODA should be considered an important criterion of contribution;

    (b) They should bring into the decision-making process countries more representative of the broader membership, especially of the developing world;

(c) They should not impair the effectiveness of the Security Council;

(d) They should increase the democratic and accountable nature of the body.

170. I urge Member States to consider the two options, models A and B, proposed in that report (see box 5), or any other viable proposals in terms of size and balance that have emerged on the basis of either model. Member States should agree to take a decision on this important issue before the summit in September 2005. It would be very preferable for Member States to take this vital decision by consensus, but if they are unable to reach consensus this must not become an excuse for postponing action.

Box 5

Security Council reform: models A and B

Model A provides for six new permanent seats, with no veto being created, and three new two-year-term non-permanent seats, divided among the major regional areas as follows:

Regional area	Number of States	Permanent seats (continuing)	Proposed new permanent seats	Proposed two-year seats (non-renewable)	Total
Africa	53	0	2	4	6
Asia and Pacific	56	1	2	3	6
Europe	47	3	1	2	6
Americas	35	1	1	4	6
Totals model A	191	5	6	13	24

Model B provides for no new permanent seats but creates a new category of eight four-year renewable-term seats and one new two-year non-permanent (and non-renewable) seat, divided among the major regional areas as follows:

Regional area	Number of States	Permanent seats (continuing)	Proposed new permanent seats	Proposed two-year seats (non-renewable)	Total
Africa	53	0	2	4	6
Asia and Pacific	56	1	2	3	6
Europe	47	3	2	1	6
Americas	35	1	2	3	6
Totals model B	191	5	8	11	24

Economic and Social Council

171. The Charter of the United Nations gives the Economic and Social Council a range of important functions that involve coordination, policy review and policy dialogue. Most of these seem more critical than ever in this age of globalization, in which a comprehensive United Nations development agenda has emerged from the summits and conferences of the 1990s. More than ever, the United Nations needs to be able to develop and implement policies in this area in a coherent manner. The functions of the Council are generally thought to be uniquely relevant to these challenges, but it has not as yet done justice to them.

172. In 1945, the framers of the Charter did not give the Economic and Social Council enforcement powers. Having agreed at Bretton Woods in the previous year to create powerful international financial institutions and expecting that these would be complemented by a world trade organization in addition to the various specialized agencies, they clearly intended that international economic decision-making would be decentralized. But this only makes the Council's potential role as coordinator, convener, forum for policy dialogue and forger of consensus the more important. It is the only organ of the United Nations explicitly mandated by the Charter to co-ordinate the activities of the specialized agencies and to consult with non-governmental organizations. And it has a network of functional and regional commissions operating under its aegis which are increasingly focused on the implementation of development goals.

173. The Economic and Social Council has put these assets to good use in the recent years, building bridges through an annual special high-level meeting with the trade and financial institutions, for instance, and establishing a unique Information and Communications Technology Task Force. It has also contributed to linking the issues of security and development by establishing country-specific groups.

174. These initiatives have helped to promote greater coherence and coordination among various actors, but there are still visible gaps to be addressed.

175. First, there is an increasing need to integrate, coordinate and review the implementation of the United Nations development agenda that has emerged from the world conferences and summits. **To this end, the Economic and Social Council should hold annual ministerial-level assessments of progress towards agreed development goals, particularly the Millennium Development Goals.** These assessments could be based on peer reviews of progress reports prepared by member States, with support from United Nations agencies and the regional commissions.

176. Second, there is a need to review trends in international development cooperation, promote greater coherence among the development activities of different actors and strengthen the links between the normative and operational work of the United Nations system. **To address this gap, the Economic and Social Council should serve**

as a high-level development cooperation forum. Such a forum could be held biennially by transforming the high-level segment of the Council.

177. Third, there is a need to address economic and social challenges, threats and crises as and when they occur. **To this end, the Council should convene timely meetings, as required, to assess threats to development, such as famines, epidemics and major natural disasters, and to promote coordinated responses to them.**

178. Fourth, there is a need to systematically monitor and deal with the economic and social dimensions of conflicts. The Economic and Social Council has tried to fulfil this need by establishing country-specific ad hoc advisory groups. But given the scale and the challenge of long-term recovery, reconstruction and reconciliation, ad hoc arrangements are not enough. **The Economic and Social Council should institutionalize its work in post-conflict management by working with the proposed Peacebuilding Commission. It should also reinforce its links with the Security Council in order to promote structural prevention.**

179. Finally, while the normative and strategy-setting role of the Economic and Social Council is clearly different from the managerial and policy-making role played by the governing bodies of the various international institutions, I would hope that, as the Council starts to assert leadership in driving a global development agenda, it will be able to provide direction for the efforts of the various intergovernmental bodies in this area throughout the United Nations system.

180. Implementing all these recommendations would require the Economic and Social Council to function with a new and more flexible structure, not necessarily restricted by the current annual calendar of "segments" and "substantive session". In addition, the Council needs an effective, efficient and representative intergovernmental mechanism for engaging its counterparts in the institutions dealing with finance and trade. This could be achieved either by expanding its Bureau or by establishing an Executive Committee with a regionally balanced composition.

Proposed Human Rights Council

181. The Commission on Human Rights has given the international community a universal human rights framework, comprising the Universal Declaration on Human Rights, the two International Covenants[21] and other core human rights treaties. During its annual session, the Commission draws public attention to human rights issues and debates, provides a forum for the development of United Nations human rights policy and establishes a unique system of independent and expert special procedures to observe and analyse human rights compliance by theme and by country. The Commission's close engagement with hundreds of civil society organizations provides an opportunity for working with civil society that does not exist elsewhere.

182. Yet the Commission's capacity to perform its tasks has been increasingly undermined by its declining credibility and professionalism. In particular, States have

sought membership of the Commission not to strengthen human rights but to protect themselves against criticism or to criticize others. As a result, a credibility deficit has developed, which casts a shadow on the reputation of the United Nations system as a whole.

183. **If the United Nations is to meet the expectations of men and women everywhere — and indeed, if the Organization is to take the cause of human rights as seriously as those of security and development — then Member States should agree to replace the Commission on Human Rights with a smaller standing Human Rights Council.** Member States would need to decide if they want the Human Rights Council to be a principal organ of the United Nations or a subsidiary body of the General Assembly, but in either case its members would be elected directly by the General Assembly by a two-thirds majority of members present and voting. The creation of the Council would accord human rights a more authoritative position, corresponding to the primacy of human rights in the Charter of the United Nations. Member States should determine the composition of the Council and the term of office of its members. Those elected to the Council should undertake to abide by the highest human rights standards.

C. The Secretariat

184. A capable and effective Secretariat is indispensable to the work of the United Nations. As the needs of the Organization have changed, so too must the Secretariat. That is why in 1997 I launched a package of structural reforms for the Secretariat and followed up with a further set of managerial and technical improvements in 2002, aimed at giving the Organization a more focused work programme and a simpler system of planning and budgeting and enabling the Secretariat to provide better service.

185. I am glad that the General Assembly has given broad support to these changes and I believe they have improved our ability to do the job the world expects of us. Thanks to changes in budgeting, procurement, human resources management and the way peacekeeping missions are supported, we now do business in a new and different way. But these reforms do not go far enough. If the United Nations is to be truly effective, the Secretariat will have to be completely transformed.

186. Those with the power to make decisions — essentially the General Assembly and the Security Council — must take care, when they assign mandates to the Secretariat, that they also provide resources adequate for the task. In return, management must be made more accountable and the capacity of intergovernmental bodies to oversee it must be strengthened. The Secretary-General and his or her managers must be given the discretion, the means, the authority and the expert assistance that they need to manage an organization which is expected to meet fast-changing operational needs in many different parts of the world. Similarly, Member States must

have the oversight tools that they need to hold the Secretary-General truly accountable for his/her strategy and leadership.

187. Member States also have a central role to play in ensuring that the Organization's mandates stay current. **I therefore ask the General Assembly to review all mandates older than five years to see whether the activities concerned are still genuinely needed or whether the resources assigned to them can be reallocated in response to new and emerging challenges.**

188. Today's United Nations staff must be: (a) aligned with the new substantive challenges of the twenty-first century; (b) empowered to manage complex global operations; and (c) held accountable.

189. First, I am taking steps to realign the Secretariat's structure to match the priorities outlined in the present report. This will entail creating a peacebuilding support office and strengthening support both for mediation (my "good offices" function) and for democracy and the rule of law. In addition, I intend to appoint a Scientific Adviser to the Secretary-General, who will provide strategic forward-looking scientific advice on policy matters, mobilizing scientific and technological expertise within the United Nations system and from the broader scientific and academic community.

190. Achieving real progress in new areas requires staff with the skills and experience to address new challenges. It also requires a renewed effort to secure "the highest standards of efficiency, competence and integrity", as required by Article 101.3 of the Charter of the United Nations, while "recruiting the staff on as wide a geographical basis as possible" and, we must add today, ensuring a just balance between men and women. While existing staff must have reasonable opportunities to develop within the Organization, we cannot continue to rely on the same pool of people to address all our new needs. **I therefore request the General Assembly to provide me with the authority and resources to pursue a one-time staff buyout so as to refresh and realign the staff to meet current needs.**

191. Second, the Secretariat must be empowered to do its work. The High-level Panel suggested that I appoint a second Deputy Secretary-General to improve the decision-making process on peace and security. Instead, I have decided to create a cabinet-style decision-making mechanism (with stronger executive powers than the present Senior Management Group) to improve both policy and management. It will be supported by a small cabinet secretariat to ensure the preparation and follow-up of decision-making. In this way, I expect to be able to ensure more focused, orderly and accountable decision-making. This should help but will not by itself be enough to ensure the effective management of the worldwide operations of such a complex Organization. The Secretary-General, as Chief Administrative Officer of the Organization, must be given a higher level of managerial authority and flexibility. He or she needs to have the ability to adjust the staffing table as necessary

and without undue constraint. And our administrative system needs to be thoroughly modernized. **Therefore, I ask Member States to work with me to undertake a comprehensive review of the budget and human resources rules under which we operate.**

192. Third, we must continue to improve the transparency and accountability of the Secretariat. The General Assembly has taken an important step towards greater transparency by making internal audits available to Member States upon request. I am in the process of identifying other categories of information that could be made available routinely. I am establishing a Management Performance Board to ensure that senior officials are held accountable for their actions and the results their units achieve. A number of other internal improvements are under way. These aim to align our management systems and human resource policies with the best practices of other global public and commercial organizations. **In order to further improve accountability and oversight, I have proposed that the General Assembly commission a comprehensive review of the Office of Internal Oversight Services with a view to strengthening its independence and authority as well as its expertise and capacity.** I hope the Assembly will act promptly on this proposal.

D. SYSTEM COHERENCE

193. Beyond the Secretariat, the United Nations system of funds, programmes and specialized agencies brings together a unique wealth of expertise and resources, encompassing the full spectrum of global issues. And what is true for the United Nations proper is valid also for the other parts of the system. All must be clearly accountable to both their governing bodies and the people they serve.

194. Over the past few decades, responding to steadily growing demand, the system has seen a welcome expansion in its membership as well as in the scale and scope of its activities. One unfortunate side effect of this has been that there is now often significant duplication of mandates and actions between different bodies within the system. Another has been significant shortfalls in necessary funding.

195. To try to address some of these problems I have launched two sets of major reforms during my time as Secretary-General. First, in my 1997 report, entitled "Renewing the United Nations: a programme for reform" (A/51/950), I introduced several measures, including notably the creation of executive committees, to strengthen the leadership capacity of the Secretariat and provide better coordination in the humanitarian and development fields. Then in 2002, in a second report, entitled "Strengthening the United Nations: an agenda for further change" (A/57/387 and Corr.1), I set out further steps aimed more directly at improving our work at the country level, particularly by strengthening the resident coordinator system. I have also given more authority to my special representatives and instituted a system of integrated peace operations.

196. These efforts have paid significant dividends by enabling the various agencies to work more closely together at the country level, both with each other and with other partners, such as the World Bank. Nevertheless, the United Nations system as a whole is still not delivering services in the coherent, effective way that the world's citizens need and deserve.

197. Part of the problem is clearly related to the structural constraints we face. In the medium and longer term, we will need to consider much more radical reforms to address these. Such reforms could include grouping the various agencies, funds and programmes into tightly managed entities, dealing respectively with development, the environment and humanitarian action. And this regrouping might involve eliminating or merging those funds, programmes and agencies which have complementary or overlapping mandates and expertise.

198. Meanwhile, there are more immediate actions that we can and should take now. In particular, I am introducing further improvements in the coordination of the United Nations system presence and performance at the country level, based on a simple principle: at every stage of United Nations activities, the senior United Nations official present in any given country — special representative, resident coordinator or humanitarian coordinator — should have the authority and resources necessary to manage an integrated United Nations mission or "country presence" so that the United Nations can truly function as one integrated entity.

The United Nations at the country level

199. In every country where the United Nations has a development presence, United Nations agencies, funds and programmes should organize their technical efforts to help that country develop and implement the national Millennium Development Goals–based poverty reduction strategies set out in section II above. While the management of the resident coordinator system should remain with the United Nations Development Programme (UNDP), which is our principal development institution, the broader United Nations Development Group (UNDG) should guide resident United Nations country teams, led by properly resourced and empowered resident coordinators. The United Nations Development Assistance Framework should identify a clear set of strategic objectives and define the specific assistance that each United Nations entity must give to help our national partners achieve the Goals and meet their broader development needs. Governments and the United Nations itself can then use this "results matrix" to monitor and assess the performance of the United Nations system at the country level and hold its representatives accountable.

Strengthening the resident coordinator system

200. To drive this process, I shall further strengthen the role of my resident coordinators, giving them more authority so that they can coordinate better. But the governing

boards of different agencies also need to provide guidance to support this process. **I call on Member States to coordinate their representatives on these governing boards so as to make sure that they pursue a coherent policy in assigning mandates and allocating resources throughout the system.** I also urge Member States to increase core funding and reduce the proportion of earmarked funds so as to help increase coherence in the system. As mentioned above, I hope a reinvigorated Economic and Social Council will give overall direction to this new coherence.

201. In recent years, I have been gratified by the benefits that the United Nations system has derived from working closely with independent scientists, policy makers and political leaders around the world. This is particularly true in the field of development, where we need constantly to integrate the latest advances in science and technology into the practice of our organizations and programmes. In 2005, to consolidate the links between United Nations development efforts and the world's leading minds in relevant fields, I intend to launch a Council of Development Advisers. This Council, working in close cooperation with the Secretary-General's Scientific Adviser mentioned above, will comprise some two dozen people, who should represent a cross section of leading world scientists, policy-making officials and political leaders. They will advise both me and UNDG on the best ways to support the achievement of the Millennium Development Goals, will issue periodic reports and commentaries, and will liaise with scientific, civil society and other bodies with relevant expertise. Their advice will also be available to the Economic and Social Council.

Humanitarian response system

202. From the Indian Ocean tsunami to the crises in Darfur and the eastern Democratic Republic of the Congo, recent months have provided eloquent testimony to the ever-growing range and scale of demands being placed on the international humanitarian response system. With leadership and coordination from the United Nations, the system that comprises the humanitarian community of agencies and non-governmental organizations has been performing reasonably well, under the circumstances. Expert humanitarian workers get deployed and large quantities of food and other relief items are now provided to victims of war and natural disasters anywhere in the world within a matter of days. There is less overlap between agencies and a more effective coordination between non-governmental and inter-governmental actors on the ground.

203. The system was able to provide massive relief to all tsunami-affected communities in the Indian Ocean, against all odds, in the course of a few weeks. Yet at the same time, assistance to displaced people in Darfur is falling well short of what had been pledged, while major crises, such as the one in the Democratic Republic of Congo, where more than 3.8 million people have been killed and 2.3 million displaced since 1997, remain woefully underfunded. Humanitarian response needs to become more

predictable in all emergencies. To achieve that, we need to make rapid progress on three fronts.

204. First, the humanitarian system needs to have a more predictable response capacity in areas where now there too often are gaps, ranging from the provision of water and sanitation to shelter and camp management. When crises are already under way, there is a need to operate quickly and flexibly. This is particularly the case in complex emergencies, during which humanitarian requirements are linked to the dynamics of conflict and circumstances can change rapidly. In general, it is the relevant United Nations country team, under the leadership of the humanitarian coordinator, which is best placed to identify the opportunities and constraints. However, there is a clear need to strengthen field coordination structures, notably by better preparing and equipping United Nations country teams, strengthening the leadership of the humanitarian coordinator and ensuring that sufficient and flexible resources are immediately available to support these field structures.

205. Second, we need predictable funding to meet the needs of vulnerable communities. We need to ensure that the generous outpouring of global support to the tsunami crisis becomes the rule, not the exception. This means building on the humanitarian community's work with the donor community and more systematically engaging with new donor Governments and the private sector. Ensuring consistent and timely responses to crises requires both that pledges be rapidly converted into tangible resources and that more predictable and flexible funding be made available for humanitarian operations, particularly in the initial emergency phases.

206. Third, we need to have a predictable right of access and guaranteed security for our humanitarian workers and operations in the field. Humanitarian personnel are too often blocked from providing assistance because government forces or armed groups prevent them from doing their jobs. Elsewhere, terrorists attack our unarmed aid workers and paralyse operations, in violation of basic international law.

207. I am working with my Emergency Relief Coordinator to address these issues and to come up with concrete recommendations for strengthened action. A comprehensive humanitarian response review is currently under way and its findings will be made available in June 2005. **I expect them to include a series of proposals for new standby arrangements for personnel and equipment to ensure the capacity to respond immediately to major disasters and other emergencies, if need be in several areas at the same time.** I shall work with Member States and agencies to ensure that these proposals, once finalized, will be implemented without delay.

208. To enable immediate response to sudden disasters or large unmet needs in neglected emergencies, we need to consider the adequacy of the financial tools at our disposal. **We should examine whether the existing Central Emergency Revolving Fund should be upgraded or a new funding mechanism should be established.** In the latter case, the proposal put forward by donors to set up a $1 billion voluntary fund deserves serious consideration.

209. Special attention is due to the growing problem of internally displaced persons. Unlike refugees, who have crossed an international border, those displaced within their own countries by violence and war are not protected by established minimum standards.

210. Yet this acutely vulnerable group now totals roughly 25 million, more than double the estimated number of refugees. **I urge Member States to accept the Guiding Principles on Internal Displacement (E/CN.4/1998/53/Add.2) prepared by my Special Representative as the basic international norm for protection of such persons, and to commit themselves to promote the adoption of these principles through national legislation.** Unlike refugees, who are looked after by the Office of the United Nations High Commissioner for Refugees, internally displaced persons and their needs often fall into the cracks between different humanitarian bodies. Recent steps have been taken to ensure that agencies provide assistance to such groups within their respective areas of competence, on a collaborative basis. But, as we have seen most recently in Darfur, more is needed. **I intend to strengthen further the inter-agency response to the needs of internally displaced persons, under the global leadership of my Emergency Relief Coordinator, and at the country level through the humanitarian coordinator system. I trust that Member States will support me in this effort.**

211. Finally, I intend to call more systematically on Member States in general and the Security Council in particular to address the unacceptable humanitarian access blockages that we are too often facing. **In order to save unnecessary pain and suffering, it is essential to protect humanitarian space and ensure that humanitarian actors have safe and unimpeded access to vulnerable populations.** I shall also take measures, through the newly established Secretariat Department of Safety and Security, to make our risk management system more robust so that humanitarian workers can undertake their life-saving operations in high-risk areas without unduly endangering their own lives.

Governance of the global environment

212. Given the number and complexity of international agreements and agencies that cover it, the environment poses particular challenges to coherence. There are now more than 400 regional and universal multilateral environmental treaties in force, covering a broad range of environmental issues, including biodiversity, climate change and desertification. The sectoral character of these legal instruments and the fragmented machinery for monitoring their implementation make it harder to mount effective responses across the board. There is a clear need to streamline and consolidate our efforts to follow up and implement these treaties. Already in 2002, the World Summit on Sustainable Development, held in Johannesburg, emphasized the need for a more coherent institutional framework of international environmental governance, with better coordination and monitoring. **It is now high time to consider a more integrated structure for environmental standard-setting, sci-**

entific discussion and monitoring treaty compliance. This should be built on existing institutions, such as the United Nations Environment Programme, as well as the treaty bodies and specialized agencies. Meanwhile, environmental activities at the country level should benefit from improved synergies, on both normative and operational aspects, between United Nations agencies, making optimal use of their comparative advantages, so that we have an integrated approach to sustainable development, in which both halves of that term are given their due weight.

E. Regional organizations

213. A considerable number of regional and subregional organizations are now active around the world, making important contributions to the stability and prosperity of their members, as well as of the broader international system. The United Nations and regional organizations should play complementary roles in facing the challenges to international peace and security. **In this connection, donor countries should pay particular attention to the need for a 10-year plan for capacity-building with the African Union.** To improve coordination between the United Nations and regional organizations, within the framework of the Charter of the United Nations, I intend to introduce memorandums of understanding between the United Nations and individual organizations, governing the sharing of information, expertise and resources, as appropriate in each case. For regional organizations that have a conflict prevention or peacekeeping capacity, these memorandums of understanding could place those capacities within the framework of the United Nations Standby Arrangements System.

214. I also intend to invite regional organizations to participate in meetings of United Nations system coordinating bodies, when issues in which they have a particular interest are discussed.

215. **The rules of the United Nations peacekeeping budget should be amended to give the United Nations the option, in very exceptional circumstances, to use assessed contributions to finance regional operations authorized by the Security Council, or the participation of regional organizations in multi-pillar peace operations under the overall United Nations umbrella.**

F. Updating the Charter of the United Nations

216. As I remarked at the beginning of section V, the principles of the Charter of the United Nations remain fully valid, and the Charter itself, in the main, continues to provide a solid foundation for all our work. It is still essentially the document that was drafted at the San Francisco Conference six decades ago. Much has been achieved by changes in practice without the need for amendment. In fact, the Charter has been amended only twice during the history of the Organization — for the

purpose of enlarging the membership of the Security Council and the Economic and Social Council.

217. Nonetheless, the United Nations now operates in a radically different world from that of 1945, and the Charter should reflect the realities of today. **In particular, it is high time to eliminate the anachronistic "enemy" clauses in Articles 53 and 107 of the Charter.**

218. The Trusteeship Council played a vital role in raising standards of administration in the Trust Territories and promoting the wider process of decolonization. But its work is long since complete. **Chapter XIII, "The Trusteeship Council", should be deleted from the Charter.**

219. **For similar reasons, Article 47 on the Military Staff Committee should be deleted, as should all references to this Committee in Articles 26, 45 and 46.**

VI. Conclusion: our opportunity and our challenge

VI. Conclusion: our opportunity and our challenge

220. At no time in human history have the fates of every woman, man and child been so intertwined across the globe. We are united both by moral imperatives and by objective interests. We can build a world in larger freedom — but to do it we must find common ground and sustain collective action. This task can seem daunting, and it is easy to descend into generalities or stray into areas of such deep disagreement that differences are reinforced, not overcome.

221. Yet it is for us to decide whether this moment of uncertainty presages wider conflict, deepening inequality and the erosion of the rule of law, or is used to renew our common institutions for peace, prosperity and human rights. Now is the time to act. Enough words and good intentions: in the present report I have largely limited myself to the decisions that I believe are both needed and achievable in 2005. In the annex, I have listed a number of specific items for consideration by Heads of State and Government.

222. To make the right choice, leaders will need what United States President Franklin D. Roosevelt, whose vision was so central to the founding of the United Nations, called "the courage to fulfil [their] responsibilities in an admittedly imperfect world".[22] They will also need the wisdom to transcend their differences. Given firm, clear-sighted leadership, both within States and among them, I am confident that they can. I am also certain that they must. What I have called for here is possible. It is within reach. From pragmatic beginnings could emerge a visionary change of direction in our world. That is our opportunity and our challenge.

Annex

Annex

For decision by Heads of State and Government

1. The Summit will be a unique opportunity for the world's leaders to consider a broad range of issues and make decisions that will improve the lives of people around the world significantly. This is a major undertaking — one worthy of the world's leaders collectively assembled.

2. In the twenty-first century, all States and their collective institutions must advance the cause of larger freedom — by ensuring freedom from want, freedom from fear and freedom to live in dignity. In an increasingly interconnected world, progress in the areas of development, security and human rights must go hand in hand. There will be no development without security and no security without development. And both development and security also depend on respect for human rights and the rule of law.

3. No State can stand wholly alone in today's world. We all share responsibility for each other's development and security. Collective strategies, collective institutions and collective action are indispensable.

4. Heads of State and Government must therefore agree on the nature of the threats and opportunities before us and take decisive action.

I. FREEDOM FROM WANT

5. In order to reduce poverty and promote global prosperity for all, I urge Heads of State and Government to:

   (a) Reaffirm, and commit themselves to implementing, the development consensus based on mutual responsibility and accountability agreed in 2002 at the International Conference on Financing for Development held in Monterrey, Mexico, and the World Summit on Sustainable Development held in Johannesburg, South Africa. Consistent with that historic compact, centred on the Millennium Development Goals:

      (i) Developing countries should recommit themselves to taking primary responsibility for their own development by strengthening governance, combating corruption and putting in place the policies and investments to drive private sector–led growth and maximize domestic resources to fund national development strategies;

      (ii) Developed countries should undertake to support these efforts through increased development assistance, a more development-oriented trade system and wider and deeper debt relief;

(b)   Recognize the special needs of Africa and reaffirm the solemn commitments made to address those needs on an urgent basis;

(c)   Decide that each developing country with extreme poverty should by 2006 adopt and begin to implement a comprehensive national strategy bold enough to meet the Millennium Development Goals targets for 2015;

(d)   Undertake to ensure that developed countries that have not already done so establish timetables to achieve the target of 0.7 per cent of gross national income for official development assistance by no later than 2015, starting with significant increases no later than 2006 and reaching at least 0.5 per cent by 2009;

(e)   Decide that debt sustainability should be redefined as the level of debt that allows a country to both achieve the Millennium Development Goals and reach 2015 without an increase in its debt ratios; that, for most HIPC countries, this will require exclusively grant-based finance and 100 per cent debt cancellation, while for many heavily indebted non-HIPC and middle-income countries it will require significantly more debt reduction than has yet been on offer; and that additional debt cancellation should be achieved without reducing the resources available to other developing countries and without jeopardizing the long-term financial viability of international financial institutions;

(f)   Complete the World Trade Organization Doha round of multilateral trade negotiations no later than 2006, with full commitment to realizing its development focus, and as a first step provide immediate duty-free and quota-free market access for all exports from the least developed countries;

(g)   Decide to launch, in 2005, an International Financial Facility to support an immediate front-loading of official development assistance, underpinned by commitments to achieving the 0.7 per cent ODA target no later than 2015, and to consider other innovative sources of finance for development to supplement the Facility in the longer term;

(h)   Decide to launch a series of "quick win" initiatives so as to realize major immediate progress towards the Millennium Development Goals through such measures as the free distribution of malaria bed nets and effective antimalaria medicines, the expansion of home-grown school meals programmes using locally produced foods and the elimination of user fees for primary education and health services;

(i)   Ensure that the international community urgently provides the resources needed for an expanded and comprehensive response to HIV/AIDS, as identified by UNAIDS and its partners, and full funding for the Global Fund to Fight AIDS, Tuberculosis and Malaria;

(j)   Reaffirm gender equality and the need to overcome pervasive gender bias by increasing primary school completion and secondary school access for girls, ensuring secure tenure of property to women, ensuring access to reproductive health services, promoting equal access to labour markets, providing opportunity for greater representation in government decision-making bodies, and supporting direct interventions to protect women from violence;

(k)   Recognize the need for significantly increased international support for scientific research and development to address the special needs of the poor in the areas of health, agriculture, natural resource and environmental management, energy and climate;

(l)   Ensure concerted global action to mitigate climate change, including through technological innovation, and therefore resolve to develop a more inclusive international framework for climate change beyond 2012, with broader participation by all major emitters and both developing and developed countries, taking into account the principle of common but differentiated responsibilities;

(m)   Resolve to establish a worldwide early warning system for all natural hazards, building on existing national and regional capacity;

(n)   Decide that, starting in 2005, developing countries that put forward sound, transparent and accountable national strategies and require increased development assistance should receive a sufficient increase in aid, of sufficient quality and arriving with sufficient speed to enable them to achieve the Millennium Development Goals.

II. Freedom from fear

6.   In order to provide effective collective security in the twenty-first century, I urge Heads of State and Government to pledge concerted action against the whole range of threats to international peace and security, and in particular to:

(a)   Affirm and commit themselves to implementing a new security consensus based on the recognition that threats are interlinked, that development, security and human rights are mutually interdependent, that no State can protect itself acting entirely alone and that all States need an equitable, efficient and effective collective security system; and therefore commit themselves to agreeing on, and implementing, comprehensive strategies for confronting the whole range of threats, from international war through weapons of mass destruction, terrorism, State collapse and civil conflict to deadly infectious disease, extreme poverty and the destruction of the environment;

(b)   Pledge full compliance with all articles of the Treaty on the Non-Proliferation of Nuclear Weapons, the Biological and Toxin Weapons Convention, and the

Chemical Weapons Convention in order to further strengthen the multilateral framework for non-proliferation and disarmament, and in particular:

(i) Resolve to bring to an early conclusion negotiations on a fissile material cut-off treaty;

(ii) Reaffirm their commitment to a moratorium on nuclear test explosions and to the objective of the entry into force of the Comprehensive Nuclear-Test-Ban Treaty;

(iii) Resolve to adopt the Model Additional Protocol as the norm for verifying compliance with the Treaty on the Non-Proliferation of Nuclear Weapons;

(iv) Commit themselves to expediting agreement on alternatives, consistent with the Treaty on the Non-Proliferation of Nuclear Weapons principles of the right to peaceful uses and the obligations for non-proliferation, to the acquisition of domestic uranium enrichment and plutonium separation facilities;

(v) Commit themselves to further strengthening the Biological and Toxin Weapons Convention;

(vi) Urge all chemical-weapon States to expedite the scheduled destruction of chemical-weapon stockpiles;

(c) Develop legally binding international instruments to regulate the marking, tracing and illicit brokering of small arms and light weapons; and ensure the effective monitoring and enforcement of United Nations arms embargoes;

(d) Affirm that no cause or grievance, no matter how legitimate, justifies the targeting and deliberate killing of civilians and non-combatants; and declare that any action that is intended to cause death or serious bodily harm to civilians or non-combatants, when the purpose of such an act, by its nature or context, is to intimidate a population or to compel a Government or an international organization to do or to abstain from doing any act, constitutes an act of terrorism;

(e) Resolve to implement the comprehensive United Nations counter-terrorism strategy presented by the Secretary-General to dissuade people from resorting to terrorism or supporting it; deny terrorists access to funds and materials; deter States from sponsoring terrorism; develop State capacity to defeat terrorism; and defend human rights;

(f) Resolve to accede to all 12 international conventions against terrorism; and instruct their representatives to:

(i) Conclude a convention on nuclear terrorism as a matter of urgency;

(ii) Conclude a comprehensive convention on terrorism before the end of the sixtieth session of the General Assembly;

(g) Commit themselves to acceding, as soon as possible, to all relevant international conventions on organized crime and corruption, and take all necessary steps to implement them effectively, including by incorporating the provisions of those conventions into national legislation and strengthening criminal justice systems;

(h) Request the Security Council to adopt a resolution on the use of force that sets out principles for the use of force and expresses its intention to be guided by them when deciding whether to authorize or mandate the use of force; such principles should include: a reaffirmation of the provisions of the Charter of the United Nations with respect to the use of force, including those of Article 51; a reaffirmation of the central role of the Security Council in the area of peace and security; a reaffirmation of the right of the Security Council to use military force, including preventively, to preserve international peace and security, including in cases of genocide, ethnic cleansing and other such crimes against humanity; and the need to consider — when contemplating whether to authorize or endorse the use of force — the seriousness of the threat, the proper purpose of the proposed military action, whether means short of the use of force might reasonably succeed in stopping the threat, whether the military option is proportional to the threat at hand and whether there is a reasonable chance of success;

(i) Agree to establish a Peacebuilding Commission along the lines suggested in the present report, and agree to establish and support a voluntary standing fund for peacebuilding;

(j) Create strategic reserves for United Nations peacekeeping; support the efforts by the European Union, the African Union and others to establish standby capacities as part of an interlocking system of peacekeeping capacities; and establish a United Nations civilian police standby capacity;

(k) Ensure that Security Council sanctions are effectively implemented and enforced, including by strengthening the capacity of Member States to implement sanctions, establishing well-resourced monitoring mechanisms, and ensuring effective and accountable mechanisms to mitigate the humanitarian consequences of sanctions.

III. FREEDOM TO LIVE IN DIGNITY

7. I urge Heads of State and Government to recommit themselves to supporting the rule of law, human rights and democracy — principles at the heart of the Charter

of the United Nations and the Universal Declaration of Human Rights. To this end, they should:

(a) Reaffirm their commitment to human dignity by action to strengthen the rule of law, ensure respect for human rights and fundamental freedoms and promote democracy so that universally recognized principles are implemented in all countries;

(b) Embrace the "responsibility to protect" as a basis for collective action against genocide, ethnic cleansing and crimes against humanity, and agree to act on this responsibility, recognizing that this responsibility lies first and foremost with each individual State, whose duty it is to protect its population, but that if national authorities are unwilling or unable to protect their citizens, then the responsibility shifts to the international community to use diplomatic, humanitarian and other methods to help protect civilian populations, and that if such methods appear insufficient the Security Council may out of necessity decide to take action under the Charter, including enforcement action, if so required;

(c) Support the 2005 treaty event, focusing on 31 multilateral treaties, and encourage any Government that has not done so to agree to ratify and implement all treaties relating to the protection of civilians;

(d) Commit themselves to supporting democracy in their own countries, their regions and the world, and resolve to strengthen the United Nations capacity to assist emerging democracies, and to that end welcome the creation of a Democracy Fund at the United Nations to provide funding and technical assistance to countries seeking to establish or strengthen their democracy;

(e) Recognize the important role of the International Court of Justice in adjudicating disputes among countries and agree to consider means to strengthen the work of the Court.

IV. THE IMPERATIVE FOR COLLECTIVE ACTION: STRENGTHENING THE UNITED NATIONS

8. To make the United Nations a more effective and efficient instrument for forging a united response to shared threats and shared needs, I urge Heads of State and Government to:

(a) Reaffirm the broad vision of the founders of the United Nations, as set out in the Charter of the United Nations, for it to be organized, resourced and equipped to address the full range of challenges confronting the peoples of the world across the broad fields of security, economic and social issues, and human rights, and in that spirit to commit themselves to reforming, restructuring and revitalizing its major organs and institutions, where necessary, to enable them to respond effectively to the changed threats, needs and circumstances of the twenty-first century;

General Assembly

(b)   Revitalize the General Assembly by:

(i)   Instructing their representatives to adopt, at its sixtieth session, a comprehensive package of reforms to revitalize the General Assembly, including by rationalizing its work and speeding up the deliberative process, streamlining its agenda, its committee structure and its procedures for plenary debates and requesting reports, and strengthening the role and authority of its President;

(ii)   Resolving to give focus to the substantive agenda of the General Assembly by concentrating on addressing the major substantive issues of the day, such as international migration and the long-debated comprehensive convention on terrorism;

(iii)   Establishing mechanisms enabling the Assembly to engage fully and systematically with civil society;

Security Council

(c)   Reform the Security Council to make it more broadly representative of the international community as a whole and the geopolitical realities of today, and to expand its membership to meet these goals, by:

(i)   Supporting the principles for the reform of the Council and considering the two options, models A and B, proposed in the present report, as well as any other viable proposals in terms of size and balance that have emerged on the basis of either model;

(ii)   Agreeing to take a decision on this important issue before the summit in September 2005. It would be far preferable for Member States to take this vital decision by consensus. If, however, they are unable to reach consensus, this must not become an excuse for postponing action;

Economic and Social Council

(d)   Reform the Economic and Social Council by:

(i)   Mandating the Economic and Social Council to hold annual ministerial-level assessments of progress towards agreed development goals, particularly the Millennium Development Goals;

(ii)   Deciding that it should serve as a high-level development cooperation forum, reviewing trends in international development cooperation, promoting greater coherence among the development activities of different actors and strengthening the links between the normative and operational work of the United Nations;

(iii) Encouraging it to convene timely meetings, as required, to assess threats to development, such as famines, epidemics and major natural disasters, and to promote coordinated responses to them;

(iv) Deciding that the Council should regularize its work in post-conflict management by working with the proposed Peacebuilding Commission;

Proposed Human Rights Council

(e) Agree to replace the Commission on Human Rights with a smaller standing Human Rights Council, as a principal organ of the United Nations or subsidiary body of the General Assembly, whose members would be elected directly by the General Assembly by a two-thirds majority of members present and voting;

Secretariat

(f) Reform the Secretariat by:

(i) Endorsing the Secretary-General's request that the General Assembly review all mandates older than five years to see if the activities concerned are still genuinely needed or whether resources assigned to them can be reallocated in response to new and emerging challenges;

(ii) Agreeing to provide the Secretary-General with the authority and resources to pursue a one-time staff buyout so as to refresh and realign the staff to meet current needs;

(iii) Deciding that Member States should work with the Secretary-General to undertake a comprehensive review of the budget and human resources rules under which the Organization operates;

(iv) Endorsing the package of management reforms that the Secretary-General is undertaking to improve accountability, transparency and efficiency within the Secretariat;

(v) Commissioning a comprehensive review of the Office of Internal Oversight Services with a view to strengthening its independence and authority, as well as its expertise and capacity;

System-wide coherence

(g) Ensure stronger system-wide coherence by resolving to coordinate their representatives on the governing boards of the various development and humanitarian agencies so as to make sure that they pursue a coherent policy in assigning mandates and allocating resources throughout the system;

(h)   Commit themselves to protecting humanitarian space and ensuring that humanitarian actors have safe and unimpeded access to vulnerable populations; resolve to act on proposals to accelerate humanitarian response by developing new funding arrangements to ensure that emergency funding is available immediately; and support the Secretary-General's effort to strengthen the inter-agency and country-level responses to the needs of internally displaced persons;

(i)   Recognize the need for a more integrated structure for environmental standard-setting, scientific discussion and monitoring, and treaty compliance that is built on existing institutions, such as UNEP, as well as the treaty bodies and specialized agencies, and that assigns environmental activities at the operational level to the development agencies to ensure an integrated approach to sustainable development;

Regional organizations

(j)   Support a stronger relationship between the United Nations and regional organizations, including by, as a first step, developing and implementing a 10-year plan for capacity-building with the African Union, and by ensuring that regional organizations that have a capacity for conflict prevention or peacekeeping consider the option of placing such capacities in the framework of the United Nations Standby Arrangements System;

Charter of the United Nations

(k)   Decide to eliminate the references to "enemy States" contained in Articles 53 and 107 of the Charter of the United Nations; to delete Article 47 on the Military Staff Committee and the references to the Committee contained in Articles 26, 45 and 46; and to delete Chapter XIII on the Trusteeship Council.

Notes

[1] General Assembly resolution 55/2.

[2] *Investing in Development: A Practical Plan to Achieve the Millennium Development Goals* (United Nations publication, Sales No. 05.III.B.4); see also http://www.unmillenniumproject.org.

[3] *A Fair Globalization: Creating Opportunities for All* (Geneva, International Labour Organization, 2004).

[4] *Unleashing Entrepreneurship: Making Business Work for the Poor* (United Nations publication, Sales No. 04.III.B.4).

[5] See *Report of the International Conference on Financing for Development, Monterrey, Mexico, 18-22 March 2002* (United Nations publication, Sales No. E.02.II.A.7), chap. I, resolution 1, annex.

[6] United Nations, *Treaty Series*, vol. 1522, No. 26369.

[7] United Nations, *Treaty Series*, vol. 1954, No. 33480.

[8] See United Nations Environment Programme, Convention on Biological Diversity (Environmental Law and Institution Programme Activity Centre), June 1992.

[9] See *Report of the World Summit on Sustainable Development, Johannesburg, South Africa, 26 August–4 September 2002* (United Nations publication, Sales No. E.03.II.A.1), chap. I, resolution 2, annex, para. 44.

[10] FCCC/CP/1997/7/Add.1, decision 1/CP.3, annex.

[11] A/AC.237/18 (Part II)/Add.1 and Corr.1, annex I.

[12] United Nations, *Treaty Series*, vol. 729, No. 10485.

[13] See *Official Records of the General Assembly, Forty-seventh Session, Supplement No. 27* (A/47/27), appendix I.

[14] General Assembly resolution 2826 (XXVI), annex.

[15] See *Report of the United Nations Conference on the Illicit Trade in Small Arms and Light Weapons in All Its Aspects, New York, 9-20 July 2001* (A/CONF. 192/15), chap. IV.

[16] CD/1478.

[17] CCW/CONF.I/16 (Part I), annex B.

[18] See *The United Nations Disarmament Yearbook*, vol. 5: 1980 (United Nations publication, Sales No. E.81.IX.4), appendix VII.

[19] General Assembly resolution 217 A (III).

[20] General Assembly resolution 55/96.

[21] General Assembly resolution 2200 A (XXI).

[22] See message of the United States President to Congress dated 6 January 1945.